REGAIN

COMPETITIVENESS

Putting THE GOAL To Work

Revised Edition

Mokshagundam L. Srikanth
and
Harold E. Cavallaro, Jr.

The Spectrum Publishing Company, Inc.
Wallingford, Connecticut

Library of Congress Cataloging-in-Publication Data

Srikanth, Mokshagundam L., 1952 -
    Regaining competitiveness.

    Bibliography: p.
    1. Production management. 2. Goldratt, Eliyahu M.,
1948 -   Goal I. Cavallaro, Harold., 1953 -
II. Title.
TS155.S755 1987   658.5   87-20478
ISBN # 0-943953-00-6

Manufactured in the United States of America.
Fifth Printing - Fall 1990

Contents

Acknowledgements

We must acknowledge two groups without whom this book would not have been possible.

The first is the group from Israel, led by Dr. Eliyahu M. Goldratt, who gave us the start in this field in 1979. We had no idea at that time, that what was then a sophisticated algorithm would evolve under Eli's genius, into the new management philosophy called Synchronous Manufacturing and that the algorithm would fade into the background of this overall philosophy. We had the unique privilege of working under Eli during this exciting time. He and his brother Issachar Pascal, taught us, to put it colloquially, a thing or two about the manufacturing business and how it can be analyzed. We are proud to have been their proteges.

The second group directly responsible for this book is our clients. The material presented in this book is part of the education and training we provide. Several clients encouraged us to reorganize the material for more general use and this book is the result of this effort. To all of them we owe our thanks. Matthew Canfield and Anthony Toro, not only encouraged us but helped refine the ideas on how organizations should best approach such a basic change. To them we are particularly grateful.

Many clients and colleagues, too numerous to mention, have contributed to the refinement of the concepts and practical techniques that make up Synchronous Manufacturing.

Charles Seipold compiled the early draft copy of the book. The narrative summary is essentially all his work. Several people read the early draft versions of the book and provided us with valuable comments. Frank Sunderland was kind enough to read several versions carefully. We hope they can see in this final copy, that we did listen. Albert Cubelli edited the final text, and made it a better book to read. Dee DelGobbo edited and typeset the Revised Edition. Finally, our colleagues at Spectrum Management Group, Graham Side and Al Podzunas, have helped refine the book through constructive criticism (although it did not seem that way at times) and encouragement. They not only put up with us during this period, but took over some of our normal responsibilities and made it possible for us to complete the book in reasonable time.

Foreward

The material presented in this text is extremely relevant to the fresh look Pratt & Whitney is taking at its manufacturing operations. Today's manufacturing challenge requires placing the utmost emphasis on asset management. This requires a tool with which we can control and reduce our work-in-process inventories while at the same time improve our delivery performance.

In combination with the point-of-origin process control initiative, which will produce predictable, stable process output; the reduction of manufacturing lead times represents one means by which Pratt & Whitney manufacturing can "Regain Competitiveness".

To accomplish the significant improvements required, we must understand the nature of constraints within our manufacturing process and how best to manage them. The concepts and techniques presented here provide a foundation for learning which allows our business unit teams to achieve inventory reductions and an increased ability to accurately predict product shipment dates.

Beyond inventory management, you will also find thought-provoking challenges to our present shop measurement systems. It is crucial for us to understand the message that Throughput, Inventory and Operating Expense are the fundamental indicators of the health of a manufacturing enterprise.

Pratt & Whitney, like most of U.S. Industry, has to adjust its thinking to the fact that optimum local efficiencies may not produce the competitve edge a company is seeking.

As Pratt & Whitney strives to make a strong profitable manufacturing operation an integral element of its overall business strategy, the lessons taught here must more and more find their way into practice on our shop floors.

Bob Bescher
Vice President Manufacturing
Pratt & Whitney
United Technologies

Introduction

No one in America needs to be reminded of the dire plight of our manufacturing industries. The aging and derelict plants that mar the neighborhoods of industrial cities nationwide stand as stark testimony to our fall from the position of industrial preeminence we once occupied. Smoke-stack industries have not been the only casualties. Cutbacks and plant closings by America's large manufacturing companies in a broad spectrum of industries are no longer considered worthy of the evening news, unless the casualties are entire communities and large-sized ones at that. The trade deficit has reached alarming levels and continues to mount as we purchase manufactured products from sources outside the United States. The steady decline in the ability of our manufacturing industries to compete in the world marketplace is broad-based and deep-seated and today threatens our very standard of living.

The causes assigned to this decline have been many. But after a decade of searching for "quick fix" technological solutions and after a decade of further erosion of the manufacturing base, we seem to be coming to grips with the root problem. Professors Robert Hayes and Steven Wheelwright of the Harvard Business School, the venerable institution that has played a major role in defining and establishing the current view of managing a manufacturing business, were led by their research to conclude: [2]

"A significant part of the problem has been due to internal factors - - the practices and policies that American Management have followed in managing their companies." (p.6)

Professor Wickham Skinner, also of the Harvard Business School observed about the typical American factory: [3]

"Its management concepts are outdated, focussing on cost and efficiency instead of strategy, and on making piecemeal changes instead of changes that span and link the entire system." (p.39)

He went on to observe that:

"We have a management problem in American manufacturing today that is due to a 'mindset', rooted in the history of production management, which is now dysfunctional."(p. 277)

It was in such a climate that Dr. Eliyahu M. Goldratt and Jeff Cox introduced their book *The Goal*. [1] The book was brilliantly conceived to facilitate the authors' goals. One goal was to motivate people to critically reexamine the current management practices and policies used in manufacturing businesses. Another goal was to lay the foundation on which a viable alternative could be built.

The authors of *The Goal* were perceptive in realizing the inadequacy of overwhelming logical arguments to challenge people whose basic assumptions are steeped in decades of universally accepted practices and policies. Simply *telling* people that these sacrosanct practices and policies are invalid would not be enough; people had to be reached emotionally. To this end Dr. Goldratt and Mr. Cox chose to deliver their message in the form of a novel, where the reader could empathize with the characters in familiar situations.

Judging by the number of individuals who have read *The Goal* and the diversity of their backgrounds, the book has been a universal success. Much of this success is owed to the following things:

1. The story depicts the almost universal problems threatening the competitiveness of a broad spectrum of American manufacturing companies and similarly threatening our livelihoods.

2. The story identifies the central issue; that of a management technology of the past which once served us well, now impeding the improvements necessary to regain competitiveness.

3. The story presents a solution that can be universally applied to achieve rapid improvement in business performance.

It is possible to relate to the story emotionally, thereby creating in us a desire to emulate the success it depicts. However, it is often difficult to separate the message from the story and to apply it to our own situation. There are still questions to be answered:

- What is the fundamental problem with current management practices?
- What is the systematic solution that the story offers?
- How can we implement such an approach in our organization?

In dealing with a host of manufacturing companies we have found that the answers to these questions are far from clear to the readers of *The Goal*. Within each organization, different individuals answer these questions differently, based on their own experience and preconceptions. Clearly, there is a need to extract the message from the story, communicate it effectively to everyone in the organization and provide some means for them to begin to act on that basis.

The basic concepts were interwoven through the story. Moreover, the process of coming to grips with these concepts and using them to save the plant and regain the ability to compete, was the story itself. What we present here extracts what we believe to be that message from *The Goal* which needs to be understood by all managers in manufacturing if we are to regain competitiveness in the world marketplace.

The concepts presented in *The Goal* form the basis of a new management philosophy called **Synchronous Manufacturing.** Using the story of the Bearington plant as a case study we have presented in this book the basic concepts and methodologies of Synchronous Manufacturing, and the organizational issues involved in achieving such a basic change.

It is our expectation that this book will serve as an educational tool to further stimulate thought and focus discussion on the key issues involved in applying this approach within your organization.

We follow the same chronological sequence as the story in *The Goal*. To help you recall the major events in the story and to help you follow the arguments (even if you have not read the original story) we have included a narrative summary in Appendix A. For each major event in the story of the Bearington plant we discuss: The problem, the development of the solution, and the implementation of the solution.

These discussions are organized in such a way as to help you understand:

- The general concepts of the new management philosophy of Synchronous Manufacturing and its implications.

- The specific application of these concepts at the Bearington plant and the key issues they raise.

- The lessons for the application of these concepts in any manufacturing operation.

Systematic and comprehensive procedures have been developed for the application of these concepts in complex real-life manufacturing organizations. They include procedures for dealing with technical as well as organizational issues, from analysis of the problem to implementation of the solutions. We have briefly touched on these procedures in this book. A detailed discussion would require a book of its own and would lead us too far from the story at Bearington.[9]

How To Use
This Book

We are often asked: "What is the specific application of these concepts in our business?"

A book written without a detailed knowledge of your business, your processes and products, your organization and your strategies cannot be expected to provide a detailed answer to this all-important question. However, by following the plan outlined in the next section, you should be able to see for yourself the problems resulting from traditional management practices and how the new concepts will help address these key problems.

To develop the concepts and methodologies of the new management philosophy, Synchronous Manufacturing, in a step-by-step and logical manner, it is important to work through the chapters progressively. This will assure you of the basic understanding needed for the later chapters. Even if you have a general knowledge of this subject matter it is beneficial to review the fundamentals. It will at the least reinforce your understanding. Before you read any chapter, it is beneficial to read the summary in Appendix A of the corresponding chapter(s) in *The Goal*. This will help you relate to the events at the Bearington plant discussed in that chapter.

To help you begin to arrive at some of the specific details as they relate to you and your operation, we have constructed a series of Action Items. These Action Items are the key to obtaining the optimum benefit from this book. In order to put *The Goal* to work, you must first understand the concepts presented, and then try to apply these concepts to your environment. The discussion in the book will help you understand the concepts. The Action Items are designed to help you see and analyze the application in your operation. Solid understanding comes only through application.

In order to gain the most from this book we recommend reading it twice. As you read it through the first time, work through the Action Items superficially. This will give you an overview of the concepts and their application. Then read the book a second time, and try to work through the Action Items in as much detail as possible.

One of the major benefits of this new management philosophy is that it brings the organization together by focussing on the common goal. The ideal situation would be for your management team to work through these Action Items as a group activity. We have found that the resulting discussions can be quite lively and productive. The end result is often a better, more unified understanding of what has to be done to become more competitive and the development of an action plan to accomplish this.

Many have identified the traditional policies and practices that have been followed in managing our companies as the basic problem responsible for the loss of American competitiveness. We hope that the discussions in the following chapters, the Action Items and the vigorous discussions they generate, will serve to bring your organization to a closer understanding of which of these policies and practices contribute most to *your* competitive problems. We also hope that in the presentation of these concepts you will see a systematic way to address these issues.

A New Outlook
Is Necessary

The manufacturing sector of American industry is experiencing severe problems, particularly in competing with foreign competitors in the new global marketplace. It is finally being recognized that the core problem of our manufacturing operations is in the mindset of our managers and in the practices and policies they employ. The situation at the Bearington plant of Unico Corporation is typical of companies across America, as discussed in Chapter One. In Chapter Two, the implementation of Robotics is used to highlight the problems traditional management approaches create. Both the decision to invest in the Robot and the management of the Robot were based on conventional approaches aimed at improving cost and efficiency. Ironically they succeeded only in contributing to Bearington's competitive problems. The solution requires a new outlook.

1
*Competitveness Lost**

The story of the Bearington plant of the UniWare Division of UniCo Corporation contained in *The Goal* [1], is the story of a typical American manufacturing plant struggling for survival in a world which has become internationally competitive. Most people in manufacturing can relate to the experiences in this story. Whatever the product produced, whatever the technology used, whatever the market served, the sense of confusion and lack of control are the same. The intense foreign and domestic competition makes it even more overwhelming. And, as in the case of UniCo, it is felt at all levels.

In the frantic and chaotic world of manufacturing it seems that everything is accomplished on an emergency basis. Every order has to be expedited. From shop supervisor to senior executive, everyone is constantly "fighting fires" and everyone feels the pressure. It is not uncommon for situations to become critical. The late order that ignited the specific outburst in the story is a symptom of a more generic problem.

The Company

The UniCo company and the town of Bearington truly represent what has happened to manufacturing in America. UniCo was a company started before the turn of the century by an enterprising engineer. The products they made were among the best in the world and the company's prosperity had grown along with America. But the

* This Chapter follows Chapters 1 - 3 of <u>The Goal.</u> [1] See Appendix A-1 for a narrative summary of these chapters.

past decade had been a strange one for them. They had steadily lost their leadership position in the marketplace. Competitors, particularly from Japan, were eroding their market share by offering products of superior quality, with better features, at a lower price. It had become more and more difficult to generate the margins they needed to survive; and the pressure from the corporation to improve productivity and reduce cost had grown stronger.

Action Item 1.1

> Think about the origin and growth of your company...
> - What has happened in the last decade...
>   - To the market share?
>   - To the variety and complexity of the products?
>   - To the pressures from customers and management?

As in most American companies, the management at UniWare was faced with the demands of a competitive marketplace. Management struggled to meet the improvement objectives through many productivity programs:

- Efficiencies had been improved.
- NC Machines were in operation in a number of areas.
- Robots had been introduced to improve cost and quality.
- Quality programs had been initiated.
- Cost reduction efforts were being given high priority.

Action Item 1.2

> - List some of the major productivity programs that you have been a part of in the last five years.
> - What was the goal of each?
> - How is progress toward the goal monitored?

All of these programs had been fully justified and had met the strict requirements of UniCo for these types of projects. The project audits seemed to show that the programs were working, although, like most projects, they took longer than they should have and had shown some cost overruns. The only disturbing fact was that, in spite of all their efforts, UniWare was losing ground to its competition. The race was intensifying and they were falling further behind.

The People

The people at the Bearington plant were like manufacturing people in most companies. They were honest and dedicated people who had spent most of their career years in manufacturing with the same company. They took pride in the fact that they knew their products and processes thoroughly. In spite of the daily trials and tribulations of life on the factory floor, they enjoyed working with machines and producing products. They felt secure in their jobs and careers and were pleased with their contributions to society.

The intense global competition and the loss of their competitive position had changed all that. Their careers and their livelihoods were in jeopardy. They were in a constant state of uncertainty about the plant being sold, relocated or completely shut down. Cutbacks and layoffs were a perennial threat.

They still felt they could produce products that could compete with those produced anywhere in the world. They felt constrained in their attempts to restore their facilities and improve their products. However, they could not pinpoint the cause of their frustrations and their problems.

The impact of the demanding, chaotic nature of competitive pressures on the manufacturing people transcended their professional lives. The demands of the workplace often consumed the individual, and little time was left for family and social life.

The Town   The town of Bearington was once a prosperous and vibrant industrial town with a number of manufacturing plants, some much larger than UniWare. That was less than a decade ago. Bearington now resembled a ghost town. Most of the plants had been closed. Unable to compete with foreign and domestic competitors, they had simply gone out of business or moved to areas offering cheaper labor and better tax breaks. At first this move had been to the less developed parts of the United States. More recently, it meant moving the production base to foreign soil.

Action Item 1.3

- How has manufacturing fared in your town?
- How many plants within your corporation have been relocated in the last ten years?
- How many plants have been closed altogether and the products purchased from abroad?

On the national level, the story of UniCo - a once successful and profitable company that is no longer competitive - and the story of Bearington - a prosperous industrial town decimated by plant closings and layoffs - has been painfully and frequently repeated in various sections of the country.

Many attempts have been made to "explain" the inability of U.S. Industry to compete with foreign competitors. Among these are:

- Machinery and plants that are outdated.
- Strong and inflexible unions.
- High cost of domestic labor.
- Government subsidies and support.

A recently published survey in the Harvard Business Review,[6] on recent plant closings, dispels some of these myths. The median age of the plants at closing was fifteen years, and a third of the plants were no more than six years old at the time of closing. Fewer than twenty percent of the closed plants were plagued by militant unions or had a history of work stoppages. Direct labor accounted for a very small portion of the total costs, generally less than ten percent and in some cases as low as three percent.

If these are not the reasons, how can we account for our loss of competitive position? How can we account for the basic fact that with competent people, efficacious machinery and quality materials we cannot produce products of high and consistent quality, deliver them when promised and do so at a reasonable price? Why can't we seem to do it as well as our competition?

The Reasons   Two major reasons for the decline of manufacturing in America are emerging as we search for solutions:

1. Preoccupation with Asset Rearrangement : [2,3]
   The executives at the senior levels are preoccupied with improving the financial position of the company through asset rearrangement - acquisitions, mergers and divestitures. This is seen in the readiness with which the division would close down or sell off UniWare. There is no apparent willingness to fight it out; to roll up the sleeves, and put in the hard work to regain a competitive position.

2. Obsolete Management Tools and Techniques: [1,2,3,4,5]
   Management tools and techniques, developed and refined in the postwar years, now seem to be ineffective and may even block the solution. In the Bearington example, the obsolete management tools and techniques are seen in the familiar pressures to improve efficiencies and reduce costs.

It is this second issue which is the main subject of this book. Using the story of the UniWare plant as an example, we will help you understand possible core problems which may also be evident in your manufacturing operations. Further, we will help derive new insights and solutions for these critical problems.

Action Item 1.4

> - How is your management running the plant today compared with ten years ago?
> - What has changed?
> - Was it simply an attempt to refine and tighten up old procedures?
> - If automation has been introduced, is it automation of old methods or is it something really new?

*The Cost System--
A Major Obstacle*

The cost system is at the heart of most management control and decision-making processes today. Developed during the postwar years, this system served us well in the boom years that followed the second World War. It made us the foremost industrial nation in the world, with the highest Gross National Product and the most attractive world market. But the era of unchallenged leadership in manufacturing no longer exists. The most significant development, as Alex Rogo lamented, is the emergence of global competitors.

These competitors resemble the pioneers of U.S. Industry (such as Henry Ford and Eli Whitney) in their approach to manufacturing operations. They are almost fanatical in their efforts to fine tune the production processes, to do the thousand-and-one little things that must be done to achieve high levels of manufacturing excellence. They take actions which make sound business and manufacturing sense even though they may defy justification by our traditional cost systems.

There is a growing consensus among many in the accounting profession that the traditional cost system is due for an overhaul.[3,4,5,10] It has a number of fundamental flaws that hinder, rather than help management in the fight for industrial survival.

As developed in *The Goal* and explained in the following chapters, the major problems with the cost system are:

- The cost system is too internally oriented and insensitive to the needs of the marketplace.

- The cost system is local and strives to reduce the cost of each process and product. In striving to achieve this local optimum it actually creates a system that is far from the global optimum.

- The cost system is based on a number of invalid assumptions that will be explored in the subsequent chapters of this book.

Over the last three decades, manufacturing companies in America have relentlessly pursued an approach to improvement through cost reduction. Even on the verge of closing down, the corporation was asking UniWare to show more cost reductions and to improve efficiencies. It is this pursuit of cost as an end in itself that has been a major contributor to our current problems. The practices and policies designed with the sole focus on reducing cost, now stand in our way as we strive to be more responsive to the marketplace and be more competitive.

There is clear evidence of the problem with using cost-based concepts to control and improve manufacturing operations. Many programs undertaken during the 1980's with the explicit goal of restoring the competitive position do not meet the usual requirements of cost justification. The "Quality Is Job One" program launched by the Ford Motor Company is an example of such a program. Even though it fails to meet cost justification criteria, most of us feel that it was an excellent program. It can be argued, in retrospect, that what made such a massive program a survival need, was the strict adherence to cost-based decision making over the past several decades. The "Saturn" program that General Motors launched in the mid 1980s represents another example, where intuitive business judgments superseded the usual cost-based analysis.

Action Item 1.5

How many programs has your company undertaken in spite of cost considerations because of "intangible" reasons and the feeling that it was simply the right thing to do?

2

*The New World Needs A New Philosophy**

The world of manufacturing business had changed for UniWare but yesterday's management philosophy continued to be used. To highlight the problems inherent in the traditional management techniques, we will use the example of the Robot at the Bearington plant. The Robot was supposed to have resulted in significant productivity gains.

The consensus among manufacturing managers is that the introduction of robots will serve to bring costs down (since direct labor is reduced). This new technology is also expected to improve the quality and reliability of the process and is expected to improve the efficiencies of their operations. Once it was operational in your plant, automation probably lived up to expectations and you now have the "facts and figures" to show its positive impact. This information generally forms the basis for both internal management presentations as well as presentations at professional meetings.

Alex Rogo was on his way to present these "facts and figures" at a professional meeting in Houston. Many companies have even cited these benefits in their annual reports to prove that the company is taking the right actions to become competitive. UniCo was no exception as we will shortly see.

---

* This chapter follows Chapters 4 & 5 of <u>The Goal.</u>[1] *See Appendix A-2 for a narrative summary of these chapters.*

Action Item 2.1

> Use the major productivity programs you listed in Action Item 1.2.
> - What were the expected "cost" savings for each of those programs at the time of their approval?
> - What are the documented savings so far?

The Local Optimum vs. The Global Optimum

Most managers agree that automation has improved the production processes where it was introduced. Automation has, in fact, reduced the "costs" of these processes. Does this mean that it has improved the performance of the company as a whole? We have assumed for years that it has. Operating on this assumption, most managers ask for such local improvements from their people and the corporation undoubtedly asks for similar improvements from them. The one-thousand-and-one little things being done daily by Industrial Engineers, Shop Supervisors, and others in most plants, including the Bearington plant, are focussed on local improvements that reduce cost. In fact, without conscious thought, every activity is weighed in terms of its costs and benefits on the local level. That is why it is so unsettling to us when Jonah challenges the impact of the Robot.

Action Item 2.2

> - List some of the the small everyday kind of management decisions you and your management team have made.
> - Are cost/benefit analyses being considered in making these decisions, even if informally?

The critical management issue being challenged by Jonah is not what the Robot had done to the operational efficiency or even what the Robot had done to the standard cost of the parts. The critical management issue challenged here concerns the dichotomy between what the Robot did for the local optimum and what it did for the global optimum.

Jonah challenged Alex Rogo to consider this variance by posing these critical questions: [1] (pp. 28)

- Was more product shipped?
- Was inventory reduced?
- Was there a decrease in the workforce?

At the Bearington plant, the answer to all these questions was negative. We have found many instances of the application of new technologies in America where this has been the case. Alex Rogo's dilemma is painfully obvious and not uncommon. His management systems suggested the Robot was a good investment. Now, Jonah has stimulated his common sense and made him ask:

Is the *plant* really more productive as a result of the Robot?

Action Item 2.3

- What is your "gut" feeling about the programs you have analyzed in your plant?
- What have they contributed to make the company more competitive and profitable?

The seriousness of the situation has nothing to do with robots. We make most of our decisions the same way, based upon the local cost system. For example, when Bill Peach threatened to close UniWare, the discussion was based on the plant not being sufficiently productive. The conversation at the corporate office that morning was about productivity and all the various ways of improving it. These discussions were based on long-accepted indicators and measurements, such as the ratio of direct labor hours applied to production versus standard, direct labor hours applied to hours paid, and cost of raw materials. To Alex Rogo (and to all of us) they are familiar words and phrases. If we really understand productivity, and all of our programs are moving us to better levels of productivity, then why are we losing the competitive race?

Action Item 2.4

> - List the major goals that have been set for the manufacturing operations in your company.
> - How many of them were designed to eliminate inefficiencies and improve cost?
> - How many were designed in response to a specific need in the marketplace?
> - How many of the latter required a cost justification?

Is it possible that our current understanding of productivity is at the heart of the problem? If efforts to become competitive have not yielded the fruits that were expected maybe it is because productivity is being measured incorrectly. We will see in the next chapter of this book that this is, in fact, a major portion of our problem.

Synchronous Manufacturing --A Scientific Approach

To Alex Rogo's surprise, Jonah displayed an ability to predict the situation that existed in his plant. This foreshadows that a scientific approach to manufacturing will be revealed in subsequent chapters of *The Goal*[1]. Using the classic cause-effect relationships of the scientific method, Jonah was able to predict the effects on the Bearington plant's operation of managing to high efficiencies. For example, Jonah predicted with great certainty that their attempt to attain high efficiencies at the Robot must have resulted in high inventories and caused poor due-date performance. Of course, UniWare was plagued by these problems.

It is implied here that managing to achieve high efficiencies will, in most cases, cause high in-process inventories. In other words, one will cause the other and hence the two are interrelated.

Action Item 2.5

> * Are both high efficiencies and low in-process inventories included in the goals for your manufacturing operations?

Whenever mutually exclusive elements are included in the goals set for a manufacturing operation it will be impossible to achieve both high efficiency and low in-process inventory. When good performance is achieved with respect to one of the elements, performance relative to the other will suffer. If one is perceived as more important than the other, that will prevail at the expense of the other. In the case of the Bearington plant, efficiencies prevailed at the expense of in-process inventories.

Action Item 2.6

> Review the historical performance of the manufacturing operations in your company relative to the goals discussed in Action Item 2.4.
> * Do any of these show a pattern that suggests they are exclusive?
> * If a relationship seems to exist, identify the cause of this relationship.

The scientific method hinted at is called *Synchronous Manufacturing* and will be discussed at some length in this book. It has evolved into a science of managing manufacturing organizations encompassing well-developed procedures for classifying, understanding and improving operations.

Synchronous Manufacturing provides a new set of techniques to help evaluate and control manufacturing operations. It is a management technology more suited to today's competitive world and is free from the invalid assumptions of the cost system that we discussed in Chapter One. This book will help you understand this new approach. The basic concepts introduced in *The Goal* were interwoven through the story. In this book, we will use the story of the Bearington plant as a case study to illustrate the key concepts of Synchronous Manufacturing. We will also illustrate the systematic procedures for analysis, control and implementation that are a part of Synchronous Manufacturing.

A Set Of
Global Measurements

To begin developing an approach that is free from the narrow focus of conventional cost-based approaches to managing manufacturing operations, we must start by refocussing our sights on the overall objectives of the business. Chapter Three begins with the statement of the goal of a manufacturing business and then develops a set of operational measures that enable us to relate the specific manufacturing activities to the overall business goals without using the cost concept. This is necessary if we are to overcome the local view inherent in the cost system. In Chapter Four we revisit the Robot and see how the new operational measures revealed the fact that the Robot was not helping the Bearington plant become competitive. The new measures, global in nature and more intrinsic to the manufacturing process, afford us the possibility of developing a management approach that is not local.

3

An Old Goal
*And Some New Measurements**

Synchronous Manufacturing is a scientific approach to managing a manufacturing operation. It begins with a clearly stated goal of the manufacturing business. It recognizes the inherent complexities of manufacturing operations, with the many machines, products, personnel and all the problems and uncertainties of life in a competitive business. The basic principles for managing a manufacturing operation are derived systematically. It also helps management predict the impact of their actions on their business from the global perspective. Finally, it includes the procedures for implementation.

An Overall Goal   An understanding of Synchronous Manufacturing starts at a very basic level -- the goal of the manufacturing business.

The underlying goal of a manufacturing organization, like that of any business, is to MAKE MONEY.

This in itself is not new, although it may not always be in the forefront. In his investigation, Alex Rogo had to consider several possible goals, such as producing more products, improving quality and improving efficiencies. On close examination, these turned out to be the means to the basic goal. In reality, we are not challenging

---

*This Chapter follows Chapters 6 - 8 of The Goal.[1] See Appendix A-3 for a narrative summary of these chapters.

the ultimate goal of a manufacturing business. We are challenging the assumptions inherent in some of the intermediate steps used by management to assist in reaching the goal. We specifically challenge the assumption that making local productivity improvements, such as the Robot at the Bearington plant, will actually result in the company making money.

Bringing the overall goal of an organization into focus is not of much use by itself. To effectively use a goal, a set of measurements that can quantitatively measure progress toward that goal is also needed. How well a manufacturing business, or any business, is making money can be measured through the use of three well-defined financial measures. These are: [1] (pp. 48)

1. Net Profit (NP).
2. Return On Assets (ROA).
3. Cash Flow (CF).

A business is profitable if all three measures are positive. The business performance is improving when all three measures are increasing and increasing simultaneously! Business performance is increasing when Net Profit is increasing, Return On Assets is increasing and Cash Flow is increasing.

The Present System   It is expected that manufacturing managers will take actions which will impact the financial measures of NP, ROA and CF in a positive way. In the complex manufacturing environment it is not easy to relate everyday actions on the production floor with the financial measures. For example, when Alex asked one of the supervisors to explain what he was doing for the company in terms of these financial measures, the supervisor was perplexed and could only talk in terms of labor hours and parts per shift. These are terms of the standard cost system, and in fact, the cost system is used as the bridge from manufacturing activities to the financial measures today.

Action Item 3.1

> Review the major capital and project approval procedures used in your company.
> *   How are you expected to calculate the benefits?

The standard cost system provides a detailed procedure for calculating the cost savings of any proposed action. Consider for example, a proposal to purchase a new piece of equipment, which is expected to reduce the amount of direct labor hours required at this operation.

The usual way of calculating the savings expected as a result of the new machine is as follows:

$$\text{SAVINGS IN DIRECT LABOR} =$$
$$\{\text{REDUCTION IN PROCESSING TIME}\}$$
$$\text{X }\{\text{NUMBER OF PIECES PRODUCED PER YEAR}\}$$
$$\text{X }\{\text{COST OF DIRECT LABOR}\}$$

This is then converted into a total savings through the use of appropriate overhead factors.

$$\text{TOTAL ANNUAL COST SAVINGS} =$$
$$\{\text{SAVINGS IN DIRECT LABOR}\}$$
$$\text{X }\{\text{OVERHEAD FACTOR}\}$$

While some of the details of these procedures change from company to company, the principle is the same.

Action Item 3.2

> How would your current procedures account for the following:
> - The cost of having workers standing idle?
> - The cost of producing a specific product?

The standard cost system is the fundamental decision-making technique in use today. If we review the calculations used above, we will notice that the system is local in view. By this we mean that when we are calculating the cost impact of a specific action, the rest of the plant is assumed to be unaffected by this action. This leads to the further assumption, that the calculated saving is the saving for the entire operation. A way to verify this assumption is to evaluate the impact of the same manufacturing actions on the plant directly without using the intermediate cost bridge.

A New Set of Measurements

To evaluate the impact of manufacturing actions on the plant as a whole, a set of measures are needed. Remember that cost is a local measure at the level of a process or operation. Jonah proposes an intuitive approach to developing a set of measures that can be used for the entire plant. The activities of a manufacturing operation essentially consist of the following:

- Purchase raw or partially finished material.
- Transform the material into a finished product through the use of plant resources - men and machines.
- Sell the finished product.

Using this as a basis, we can define three new measurements intrinsic to managing the flow of material:[1] (pp. 59 - 60)

1. *Throughput* (T)
   The rate at which the system generates money through sales.

2. *Inventory* (I)
   The money invested in purchasing things which it intends to sell.
3. *Operating Expense* (OE)
   The money the system spends to turn Inventory into Throughput.

Throughput, Inventory and Operating Expense are terms that are often used in manufacturing environments today. However, there are some key differences between the above definitions and the conventional usage of these terms. Throughput as defined above, is not the volume of production (measured in some set of units); it is the volume of sales (expressed in dollars). Inventory, as used traditionally, includes the "value added" element (labor and overhead, as work is performed on the materials). In the definition above, the value-added element is not included. The value of the Inventory is equal to the value of the material. As explained by Jonah, this is done to avoid the confusion created by the almost artificial distinction between direct and indirect labor and the confusion between investments in Inventory and other investments. The definition of Operating Expense includes the direct and indirect labor in the plant. Operating Expense also includes the carrying cost of the Inventory in the system.

Action Item 3.3

Answer the following questions for your manufacturing operations giving careful consideration to the new definitions:
- What is the Throughput?
- What is the Inventory ?
- What is the Operating Expense ?

If we can compute the impact of any action on these measures, which are global and natural measures of manufacturing, then we can compute the bottom line or financial impact quite easily.

Consider a manufacturing company with the financial structure described in the following example:

> NET SALES = $10 MILLION
> INVENTORY = $ 2 MILLION (BOOK VALUE)
> INVENTORY = $ 1.5 MILLION (MATERIAL VALUE)
> TOTAL ASSETS = $6 MILLION
> COST OF GOODS = $9 MILLION
> MATERIAL CONTENT OF FINISHED PRODUCT = 40%

The three financial measures have the following values:

> NET PROFIT = $1 MILLION
> RETURN ON ASSETS = 1/6 = 16.66%
> CURRENT CASH AVAILABLE = $ 1 MILLION.

What is the impact on this company of a 5% increase in Throughput, with no change in the value of Inventory and Operating Expense? A 5% increase in Throughput means an:

> INCREASE IN SALES = $0.5 MILLION

Since there is no increase in I or OE, the only additional expense involved is the purchase of the extra material. From the information above, this will be 40% of the additional sales:

> INCREASE IN MATERIAL COST = $0.2 MILLION

Therefore,

INCREASE IN NET PROFIT = $0.3 MILLION.

Since the Asset base has not changed:

RETURN ON ASSETS =
(TOTAL NET PROFIT) / (TOTAL ASSETS) =
(1.3M) / (6M) = 21.67%

The entire $0.3 million is available cash, for the company to utilize as it chooses:

INCREASE IN CASH FLOW = $0.3 MILLION

Thus, a 5% increase in Throughput, with no change in I and OE will result in:

- Increase in Net Profit of 30%.
- Increase in Return On Assets of 30%.
- Increase in Cash Flow of 30%.

A similar procedure is used to compute the impact of reducing Inventory on the financial measures. Consider, for example, a reduction in Inventory of 20%. The Throughput (sales) is unchanged. The Asset base is reduced by (0.2 x 2) = $0.4 million. With the carrying cost of 20%, the Operating Expense will be reduced by (0.2 x 0.4) = $0.08 million. All of this reduction in OE will show up as an increase in Net Profit:

INCREASE IN NET PROFIT = $0.08 MILLION.

The Return On Asset, with the new Asset base of (6 - 0.4) = $5.6 million, will be:

$$RETURN\ ON\ ASSET = (\ 1.08\ )\ /\ (\ 5.6\ ) = 19.3\%$$

The Cash Flow is increased by the additional profit as well as by the reduction in Inventory, since there will be no need to replace this Inventory. The increase from the saving in carrying cost will appear every year. The saving from reduced purchases is a one time increase only. But in the first year, the Cash Flow will increase by:

$$INCREASE\ IN\ CASH\ FLOW = (\ 0.08\ ) + (\ 0.2\ X\ 1.5\ ) = \$0.38\ MILLION$$

Thus a decrease in Inventory of 20% will impact the financial measures (relative to the original base) as follows:

Increase Net Profit by 8%.
Increase Return On Assets by 16%.
Increase Cash Flow by 38%.

Action Item 3.4

- From the information provided, what is the Operating Expense of this company?
- Calculate for the above example, the impact of reducing Operating Expense by $0.2 million.

Using The
New Measurements

How do we use these measures as a bridge? Whatever the manufacturing action proposed, we first try to determine the impact of this action on the three operational measures defined above, Throughput (T), Inventory (I), and Operating Expense (OE). This is precisely what

Jonah was asking in the initial meeting with Alex in Chicago. The three questions that Jonah wanted Alex to answer before evaluating whether the Robot had really helped Bearington's productivity were:

1. Was more product shipped?   (Did T increase?)
2. Was Inventory reduced?   (Did I decrease?)
3. Was the work force reduced?   (Did OE decrease?)

Once the impact of an action on T, I and OE are known, the impact on the financial measures can be calculated quite easily.

The operational measures of T, I and OE serve to assist in determining the impact of manufacturing actions on the financial measures. They are not a replacement for the financial measures and are not to be confused with them. Consider the example we dealt with before, the introduction of a new machine to achieve a reduction in direct labor. The traditional cost system, as we observed, enabled us to calculate the savings resulting from this action. This was assumed to be the true savings for the whole plant. The full financial impact of the decision requires other factors, such as depreciation, taxes, payment terms etc., to be considered. The procedures for translating the calculated cost savings into a full financial analysis of the new equipment purchase are also well defined within every manufacturing company.

In the Synchronous Manufacturing approach to manufacturing operations, we will not ask what the cost savings is for this specific action. We will rather ask, what is the impact of the new machine on the operational measurements of T, I, and OE? The basic rules used in answering this question will be developed in the following chapters of this book. This answer, rather than the cost savings, will serve as the basis for financial decision-making. The impact on T, I and OE in dollars, will be the impact on the plant. Using the standard procedures currently in use at that company and recognizing all other factors such as taxes, depreciation, payment terms, etc., this can be translated into a full financial analysis for the purchase of this new equipment .

Understanding Productivity -- The New Way

Now we can evaluate manufacturing actions as being productive or non-productive. For an action to be considered productive it must impact the financial measures in a positive way. Very few actions will impact all three measures of NP, ROA and CF in a positive fashion. Most often, the impact on one of the measures will be positive, and on the others it will be neutral or negative. In such a situation, the executives will have to make a decision based on the current situation of the company and the market. Synchronous Manufacturing provides us with a better way to compute the financial impact than the traditional cost-based system. It does not mean that decisions involving trade-offs will be eliminated.

Some decisions will affect all of the financial measures of NP, ROA and CF in a positive way and do so simultaneously. They do so by simultaneously increasing T, reducing I and reducing OE. There should be no doubt that these actions are productive and will help the company make money.   The compounded impact of simultaneously increasing T, reducing I, and reducing OE, on the financial measures is very significant. In the example of the preceding section, if the improvements in T, I and OE are achieved simultaneously, then:

NEW...
NET PROFIT = $1.58 MILLION, AN IMPROVEMENT OF 58%
NEW RETURN ON ASSET = 1.58 / 5.6 = 28%, AN IMPROVEMENT OF 68%
NEW CASH FLOW = 1.88, AN IMPROVEMENT OF 88%

Similarly, some of the common manufacturing practices simultaneously impact all of the financial measures negatively. There should be no doubt that these practices are counter-productive, even though the traditional cost system may indicate otherwise. One of the most effective ways in which a company can improve its ability to make money is to identify practices that impact the financial measures negatively and replace them with practices that will have a positive effect.

Note that T, I, and OE are global measurements. They relate to the operation as a whole. They also relate the production process to sales. Two of the major drawbacks of the cost system - the internal focus and the local viewpoint - are eliminated in a system based on the measurements of T, I and OE.

Action Item 3.5

Consider the major productivity programs discussed in Action Item 2.1. Select some of the individual activities planned under these programs.
- What is the impact of these activities on the T, I and OE of your manufacturing operations?

What we must now develop is a systematic procedure for determining the impact of manufacturing actions on the T, I, and OE of the operation as a whole in such a manner that the third drawback - the invalid assumptions on which the cost system is based - is also removed.

In the development of Synchronous Manufacturing, the introduction of these global operational measures represents the first major advance. The second step is the development of the rules and procedures for calculating the impact of any action on these global measures. This is the topic of the next six chapters.

4

*New Technology Cannot Save Old Philosophy**

In the language of the new operational measurements of T, I and OE introduced by Synchronous Manufacturing, we must make decisions by evaluating the direct impact of proposed actions on Throughput, Inventory and Operating Expense.

Whether the decision is one concerning the purchase of new equipment, or the management or expansion of existing equipment and facilities, or one involving alternative ways to measure performance and motivate people, the question should always remain the same - "Will this decision serve to increase T, reduce I and reduce OE simultaneously?"

The Robot -- A Great Success?

An easy way to test the effect of these measurements on the decision-making process is to apply them to a decision that has already been made and implemented. We don't need to know the rules to predict the impact of proposed actions, because reality has done the prediction for us. This is what Alex Rogo did with the Robot. Later, we will see how he could have predicted the impact the Robot would have. For now, we are interested in what actually happened. The particular example of the Robot dramatizes the differences in conclusions drawn by the traditional cost system and those drawn by the Synchronous Manufacturing approach.

* This chapter follows Chapters 9 & 10 of The Goal.¹ See Appendix A-4 for a narrative summary of these chapters.

At the Bearington plant, the Robot was considered a tremendous success from a traditional viewpoint. The efficiency and productivity of the department in which it was introduced had improved by thirty-six percent. The quality and reliability of the process had improved, even though these could not be quantified as yet. So impressive were these results that the Chairman of the corporation had planned a personal visit to Bearington to produce a video tape on Productivity and Robots.

What Has The Robot Really Done?

When the same Robot and its application were analyzed using the measures of Synchronous Manufacturing, a completely different picture emerged. The Throughput of the plant had actually decreased (past due shipments had increased), Inventory had increased (at least of those parts processed by the Robot) and Operating Expense had increased (at least by the carrying cost of this extra inventory). The Robot had contributed to a general decline in the "productivity" of the plant. It had taken the plant further away from the goal, not closer to it.

Action Item 4.1

Using the major programs in your operation that you analyzed in Action Item 2.1, determine the impact of these programs on the operational measurements:
- Throughput - Was more product shipped? (Products shipped not products produced)
- Inventory - Did the Inventory increase or decrease? (Don't forget finished goods)
- Operating Expense - Was there a real reduction in OE? (Not calculated, but actual)

At the Bearington plant, the decision to purchase the Robot was based on incorrect expectations of what it would do for the entire plant. What happened once the Robot was operational provides further insight into how local cost-based decisions can lead to actions that take a plant further away from the goal of making money. The utilization of the Robot was low in the beginning. In fact, it was lower than what would be acceptable by the division management to justify the expenditure. To increase its utilization to a satisfactory level, the Bearington managers had released more material to the floor. The Robot was then able to operate at a better level of utilization and it appeared, in the traditional cost system, that the expected cost savings would be realized. However, as discovered when trying to discern the impact of this action on T, I and OE, the policy of achieving a local optimum at the Robot through full utilization had actually resulted in losing money.

Action Item 4.2

> Select some of the major pieces of capital equipment in your plant. Review the rules used in operating these machines.
> *   What is the origin of these rules?
> *   Use historical data to correlate some of the changes in these operating rules and their impact on the operational measurements.

Here, we see the first example of a basic truth in manufacturing:

Ensuring local optimums will not necessarily ensure the global optimum.

Yet, the standard cost system implicitly assumes that local optimums will ensure the global optimum. The reason this assumption does not hold in manufacturing operations is the subject of the next chapter.

*New Ideas Meet
Some Resistance* The discussion by the Bearington plant staff, as they try to understand the new measures of T, I and OE, brings into focus the typical problems encountered when dealing with new concepts. Once they are explained, the concepts of Throughput, Inventory and Operating Expense are intuitive and seem simple and straightforward. Yet attempts at implementing these concepts are often met with skepticism based on sacrosanct traditional beliefs. The explanation of the nuances in the definition do little to help them in applying these concepts.

When Alex Rogo used the example of the Robot, the group gravitated to the pros and cons of managing this single resource differently. If they had released too much material and caused an increase in Inventory, then they would reduce the releases and bring the inventory down. Of course, they recognized that this would not enhance the appearance of the corporate measurements.

Their efforts were concentrated on curing the symptom rather than the disease. They did not know the underlying cause, so they shifted their attention to managing the effect.

Action Item 4.3

> • How has your team reacted to the programs and activities you have been jointly analyzing?
> • Is it similar to the reaction at the Bearington plant ?

The analysis of the Robot had shown Alex that managing to local efficiencies was not good for the plant. He had identified the cause. But he did not know what should be done. If he had cut back on the material to the Robot what would have been the effect on the whole company? Without understanding this, would he not just have replaced one local optimum with another?

The analysis of the real effect the Robot had at the Bearington plant shows that the traditional way of making decisions does not improve productivity.   How can we make sure that our decisions will impact the three operational measurements properly and thus improve productivity?

The answer must begin with understanding why traditional methods fail.

Managing
Complex Operations

The operational measurements of T, I and OE introduced in Synchronous Manufacturing help define the management objectives for a manufacturing operation. We still need the rules and procedures that will guide us in reaching these objectives. Chapter Five begins this process by defining the fundamental characteristics of all manufacturing operations. These are the basic characteristics that make the assumptions of the cost system invalid in all manufacturing operations. The most immediate consequence of this analysis is that in all real-life manufacturing operations, not all elements play a similar role. This concept and its implications are developed in Chapter Six, where the idea of Constraints is introduced. It is the nature of the Constraints and the nature of the interactions between Constraints and Non-Constraints that controls the behavior of an operation. This offers the possibility for classification of manufacturing operations and the development of systematic procedures. Chapter Seven discusses the problems inherent in the adoption of a different philosophy of management. The transition from understanding and knowledge to behavior and action is not an easy one. The requirements for effective transition are discussed.

5

*Basic Phenomena Of Manufacturing**

U sing the measurements of T, I and OE introduced in Synchronous Manufacturing, the analysis of the Robot's performance from the previous chapter clearly showed that it had been mismanaged. This is not at all uncommon with major capital expenditures in many companies. What is most disturbing about the exercise with the Robot (or your programs) is that the traditional system does not reveal even the basic fact that it is being used in an unproductive fashion. We must first ask the three global questions:

1. Was more product shipped?
2. Was Inventory reduced?
3. Was there a decrease in the workforce?

Only the answers to these questions will show us the true impact of manufacturing activities. Why is this the case? The traditional cost system has served well in the past. It appears to be logical and systematic and yet it seems to fail us. The answer to this basic paradox is developed through the use of an analogy. The analogy used is that of a Boy Scout hike. It is simple enough to visualize the effects, and most of us have personally experienced a hike, either in the Scouts, the military or the like. Most importantly, it has the basic phenomena that make the assumptions underlying the cost system invalid.

*This chapter follows Chapters 11 - 17 of The Goal.[1] See Appendix A-5 for a narrative summary of these chapters.

The Traditional
System
Is A Local System

Most managers in America manage their operations under the philosophy that each and every employee should manage his actions in such a way as to reduce the cost of his actions. The traditional management philosophy can be summed up in the phrase:

"The way to achieve the global optimum is to achieve local optimums at every stage."

Whenever you make a decision to use a specific batch size for a specific product you are working to the above philosophy - you are looking at this product to the exclusion of others. Whenever you select a resource among several possibilities (each capable of performing the same task) you are working to the above philosophy - you are looking at that one process. Whenever you make a decision to make the product in house or buy it from the outside you are working to this philosophy - you are looking at the cost of this one product.

Action Item 5.1

> Review the procedures used in your company for the following activities:
> - Batch Sizing.
> - Choosing primary and alternate work centers.
> - Make/Buy decisions.
> - Determining selling price.
>
> How many of the procedures analyze that one piece in isolation?

The Basic
Phenomena

The two phenomena that undermine the foundation of the local view contained in the traditional system are:

1. Dependent Events.
2. Statistical Fluctuations.

If you have resources that are required for more than one product or if you have process routings that involve more than one step then you have Dependent Events. If your operators show a normal fluctuation in their performance to work standards you have Statistical Fluctuations. If you have resources (including tooling) that occasionally break down, if you have worker absenteeism, if you have problems with your suppliers or if your market demands fluctuate then you have Statistical Fluctuations in your operations.

Action Item 5.2

- List some of the dependent events in your plant.
- List some of the major fluctuations in your plant.

The Boy Scouts Reveal Some Basic Truths

In *The Goal*[1], the Boy Scout hike is used to show the effect these two basic phenomena have on manufacturing plants by constructing an analogy between the Boy Scout troop and a manufacturing operation. Each Boy Scout represents a resource and the rate at which he can walk represents the production rate of the resource. The material being processed is the trail itself. Raw material is represented by trail that has not been walked on by any scout. Finished product is represented by trail that has been walked on by all the scouts. Work-in-process is represented by trail that has been walked on by some but not all the scouts, since it is analogous to material processed by some but not all resources. The Throughput of the system is represented by the rate at which finished product is being produced, which is the rate at which the last scout is covering the trail. The Boy Scout hike represents a system with both Dependent Events (scouts cannot pass each other) and Statistical Fluctuations (the stride and pace of the scouts fluctuates around an average rate of about two miles per hour).

Alex Rogo initially expected the hike to proceed at the average rate of two miles per hour. He realized, of course, that there would be intervals when the scouts were walking slower than expected and there would be intervals when the scouts were travelling faster than expected. He expected these effects to average out and he expected to finish the hike in the planned five hours. He was at first surprised that the scouts' progress was far below his expectation and the scouts were spread all over the countryside. After personally verifying that the scouts were doing the best they could, he reassessed the situation. Remembering the words of Jonah about the effect of the two basic phenomena, he was led to conclude that what he was witnessing was the unavoidable effect of Dependent Events and Statistical Fluctuations.

Translating these effects of slow progress and the spreading of the troop into the world of manufacturing, Alex had to conclude that since manufacturing operations were also affected by Dependent Events and Statistical Fluctuations they would show the analogous effects, namely less Throughput and more Inventories than expected. It finally began to dawn on him that perhaps this was the central cause for the difficulty he experienced both in shipping products when promised and in controlling his inventories.

The Production Dice Game

The Production Dice Game described in Appendix B provides another very simple system in which the two phenomena of Dependent Events and Statistical Fluctuations are present.

In playing the Production Dice Game, you experience a similar situation. Even though you are producing only one product in an extremely simple process flow and most of the disturbances of a normal manufacturing business (late arrival of material, quality problems, worker absenteeism, change in demand, etc.) are absent, you have difficulty meeting the shipping requirements and your inventories increase quite dramatically. Again you are experiencing the effects of Dependent Events and Statistical Fluctuations.

Action Item 5.3

> - Play the basic Dice Game and some of the variations as described in Appendix B.
> - Document and discuss your results with your group.
> - Relate the lessons from the Dice Game to specific occurrences on the floor (Along the lines of Alex Rogo's prediction that the order for 100 sub-assemblies would not ship on time).

The Fallacy Of The Balanced Plant

The hike is used to illustrate the fallacy of the traditional local philosophy as it is used in the every day management of the shop floor. Like most manufacturing executives in America, you probably believe that labor which is not being fully utilized is counterproductive. Even though this may not be of perpetual concern to the senior executives, it is of paramount concern to the shop supervisor.

Action Item 5.4

> - Review the production and labor allocation decisions made by your shop floor supervisors in the past few hours.
> - What is the prime motivating factor behind those decisions?

Considerable time and effort are spent by your operations managers at all levels to plan the requirements for people and to carefully monitor their utilization. It is believed that labor not fully utilized will expose the areas where there is an opportunity for improving efficiencies and costs. When all pockets of labor not fully utilized have been eliminated, it is presumed a balanced plant will have been achieved, operating at peak efficiency. It is further supposed that the plant will produce products at the lowest possible cost at each resource and therefore at the lowest cost for the entire operation.

The Boy Scout hike and the Production Dice Game demonstrate analogically that this is not the case at all. They show that because your plants share the two phenomena of Dependent Events and Statistical Fluctuations, reaching a balanced capacity state would be disastrous to your performance. This is a reflection of a basic truth in statistics:[1] (pp. 100)

Whenever you have dependent events, their fluctuations do not average out; they will accumulate.

The net effect is that if a plant is ever balanced, large inventories will accumulate between resources and total production will be much less than the expected average (poor due date performance and less Throughput). This is what is seen in most plants. During the beginning of the month the capacity requirements are carefully calculated and every attempt is made to adjust the available capacity to this level. Considerable effort is spent to achieve capacity balance. Toward the end of the month, driven by a desire to meet customer promises and monthly shipping budgets, this carefully "balanced" capacity is adjusted in a frantic and reactionary mode. In effect, the capacity balance is negated.

Action Item 5.5

> - Compare the "planning activities" at the beginning of each month - shipping budgets, manpower requirements, etc., with the "fire-fighting" activities at the end of the month - overtime, expediting, off-loading, etc.
> - Does your management go through such attempts at balancing and unbalancing every month?

*Lessons For The
Unbalanced Plant*

The Boy Scout troop is not really balanced. The capabilities of the scouts are different, much like the capabilities of the different resources and different labor groups in your plant. Through the different configurations of the scouts (which scout is located where) or through the different variations of the Production Dice Game the following lessons can be learned about your manufacturing operations:

1. There is no correlation between good local measurements, such as utilization and efficiencies, and the bottom line - the performance of your plant as a whole (T, I, OE). This can be seen from a comparison of the two scenarios:

   a) When the slowest resource (Herbie for the scouts or the most loaded resource in your plants) is at the end of the process, the other resources are not forced to remain idle. They can process material according to their own capabilities. However, a narrow focus on local optimums can do nothing but increase inventories, increase production lead times and increase operating expense.

   b) When the slowest resource (Herbie for the scouts or the most loaded resource in your plants) is at the beginning of the process, the other resources are forced to work at this pace. They will end up with some idle time. However, the inventories are low, the production lead time is short and the operating expense is low.

Both a) and b) have exactly the same Throughput.

2. The Throughput of your plant is controlled by the resource with the least available capacity relative to the load placed on it. If you want to increase the Throughput of your plant (make

more product that can be sold) then you must increase the capacity of this resource (by off-loading, for example).

We Must Manage
The Causes   The existence of the two inevitable phenomena of manufacturing, Dependent Events and Statistical Fluctuations, means that deviations and inefficiencies at different operations do not average out. In fact, they accumulate.

Every expediter (and we are all expediters for a good portion of the day) is trying to compensate for the effect of these accumulated deviations. Every pile of inventory that is sitting on your factory floor represents an accumulated deviation. The constant expediting, the excessive piles of inventory (and the ensuing ramifications) and the constant chaos on the factory floor are the effects of the two basic phenomena of manufacturing and the underlying philosophy of management we have generally used.

Action Item 5.6

> * How many of the fire-fighting activities that your management team undertook this month will be repeated next month?
> * Are these fire-fighting activities curing the symptom or the disease?

To become more profitable and competitive, production facilities must be transformed into smoothly functioning units where planning and control replace today's chaos. Such a state cannot be achieved by managing the effects - by trying to manage the inventories, the use of overtime, the expediting, etc. We must begin to manage the causes - the underlying philosophy of the traditional approach.

6
Bottlenecks And
Non-Bottlenecks*

The phenomena of Dependent Events and Statistical Fluctuations common to all manufacturing operations will inevitably result in an unbalanced situation. The previous chapter has demonstrated this.

The chaos and confusion that seem to prevail on the factory floor are the result of ignoring this basic fact and managing the factory as if the capacities were balanced. This was what Bearington plant management was doing. It is also what many manufacturing operations do. Only in a balanced plant does it make sense to strive to keep all of the workforce busy producing products all of the time. Otherwise the excess capacity available must be acknowledged and managed differently. Only in a balanced plant does it make sense to treat all resources the same. Only in a balanced plant does the cost concept have any chance of leading in the right direction.

But the lesson of the previous chapter is not that a manufacturing plant *cannot* be balanced. The lesson of the previous chapter is that:[1] (pp.138)

Manufacturing plants <u>should not</u> be balanced.

This chapter follows Chapter 18 of <u>The Goal</u>.[1] See Appendix A-6 for a narrative summary of these chapters.

We have seen that while appearing to be cost efficient, capacity balanced plants will manifest missed deliveries, increased inventories and the constant need for overtime. They may appear to be efficient, but are in fact extremely inefficient at servicing the market and controlling the total expense.

This is the heart of the problem with the current approach. The focus on improving operations by evaluating them individually does not promote the welfare of the entire operation. In fact, as demonstrated in the case of the Robot, it may actually contribute to a deterioration of the operation. We must recognize that: [1] (pp. 210)

The sum of local optimums is not equal to the global optimum.

We must begin to manage the business accordingly. Only when we begin to recognize the root causes of our current problems can we hope to transform the dubiously controlled chaos that is the factory floor into a smooth and controlled process.

Bottlenecks and Non-Bottlenecks

Manufacturing operations such as the one at Bearington are not capacity balanced. As Jonah pointed out, this means that different resources have different capacities relative to the demand placed on them. Some may have more capacity than required and some may have less capacity than required. Thus in any unbalanced plant - and all plants are unbalanced - we may find two types of resources: [1] (pp.138)

1. *Bottleneck Resource:*
   A resource whose available capacity is less than or equal to the capacity required to satisfy the market demand.

2. *Non-Bottleneck Resource:*
   A resource whose available capacity is greater than the capacity required to satisfy the market demand.

As used throughout this book, a *resource* is not restricted to mean a capital piece of equipment. It is used in a general sense and includes machinery, tools, fixtures, operators, setup personnel, engineers, maintenance men, etc.

Action Item 6.1

- What resources in your plant meet the requirements of a Bottleneck Resource?
- If there are no Bottlenecks does the plant still have some of the same symptoms as Bearington?
    - Difficulty in meeting customer promises.
    - High levels of Inventory.
    - Unplanned Overtime, Premium freight, etc.

Since his pace was less than what was required to cover the hike in the allotted time, Herbie was the Bottleneck in the analogy of the Boy Scouts. The rest of the scouts were Non-Bottlenecks. It was only when Alex Rogo recognized Herbie as the factor controlling the progress of the whole troop that he was able to make progress. The same is true in every operation. The process of controlling the operation begins with the recognition that the resources fall into these two distinct categories. Resources must then be classified as Bottlenecks and Non-Bottlenecks. This is the first step toward the improvement of an operation using the approach developed in *The Goal,* the approach called Synchronous Manufacturing.

Constraints And Their Role

A Bottleneck resource limits the ability to meet the demands of customers by its available capacity. Since meeting customer demand in a timely fashion was one of the major business problems at the Bearington plant, understanding this concept was important. This may not be the major business issue in every case. Hence, the concept of a Bottleneck may not always be as important. The critical point to note is that at Bearington, where Throughput was the major problem, the Bottleneck represented the constraint to their ability to make money. Since the goal of the Bearington plant and of every business is to make money, *Constraints* are critically important.

A Constraint is an element that prevents the system from making more money.

This does not have to be a Capacity Constraint, like a Bottleneck. It does not even have to be a physical element such as a resource. Consider for example, the case where the business issue is the ability to deliver products in a shorter lead time and with better reliability. For this single issue, improving the production lead times, the constraint can be one of four types:

1. *Physical Constraint*:
   An example would be the case where the setup and process times on a resource are such that the resource is at its physical limit of production. A Bottleneck is an example of a Physical Constraint. At the Bearington plant, the Bottlenecks were affecting the reliability of their promises.

2. *Logistical Constraint*:
   An example would be where the order entry system takes a few weeks and represents a significant portion of the lead time from receipt of order to shipment. Another example of a Logistical Constraint is where the material control system uses monthly order buckets, thus losing all visibility of exact requirement dates. In both cases, the lead time that can be promised to the customer is at least four weeks.

3. *Managerial Constraint:*

    An example of this type of Constraint would be a policy that determines batch sizes such as Economic Order Quantity (EOQ). The batch size calculated by this rule might be too large and thus make the production lead times excessive.

4. *Behavioral Constraint:*

    An example of such a Constraint is a tendency on the part of the shop operators to prefer the largest batch that is ahead of a work station, irrespective of due dates or priorities. Such a behavioral tendency is generally acquired as a result of reward systems that are based on the quantity of production at individual work stations. Such behavior leads to long and unpredictable lead times.

In the Bearington plant, the constraints to improved performance were related to the production operation. In a general manufacturing operation this need not be the case. The constraint can be in any function - Engineering, Sales, Purchasing. When trying to understand and manage constraints it is important to understand the *root* cause and some of the *apparent* causes. For example, a work center that processes a great variety of products may appear to be a Physical Constraint due to the number of setups required. One solution to this constraint may be to work on reducing the time involved in setup at this work center. However, a more thorough examination may reveal that the root cause for the large number of setups is a proliferation of products. This may be caused by the Engineering Group whose focus was to reduce the cost of each new product to a minimum. Standardization of products may yield far more benefits in this case than the reduction of setups. Thus, the various ways of managing constraints have differing impacts on the system.

No matter what the nature of the constraint, it limits the company's ability to make more money. It may do so by limiting the ability to gain market share or by causing a loss of market share. Alternately, it may do so resulting in high internal expenses in the form of high inventories, excessive scrap, high freight charges and the like. To improve profitability and competitiveness we must understand what the constraints are and we must manage the constraints properly. Improvements in elements that are not constraints will not result in major improvements in the operation as a whole since they are not limiting the operation's performance.

Action Item 6.2

> * What is the major business issue of your operation?
> * Can you phrase this in terms of T, I and OE?
> * Can you identify the constraint to improved performance relative to this issue?

The first step to improving business performance is to identify the constraints, and at the Bearington plant, this meant identifying the Bottlenecks. Initially, it appears that identifying resources as Bottlenecks or Non-Bottlenecks is simply a matter of compiling data and performing the necessary calculations. Most manufacturing managers receive a weekly load report showing the calculated load on each resource based on the marketing forecasts, the bill of materials, routing and other information contained in the manufacturing data base. However, most of us will encounter the same problem as the Bearington plant. The information in the data base is not as accurate as we would like, and therefore the load analysis done using this data may be of no value. The data may not be accurate because there has not been a need to maintain all of the data. Time standards, which are used in cost computations and in evaluating operator efficiencies, are reasonably accurate and may, in fact, be overstated. But the specific resource on which the operation is performed (setup times, exact location of inventories, etc.) is usually not maintained. Shop floor people know where and how the part should be run. They do not see the need to procure that information from somebody else (Data Processing). Besides, they are too busy trying to make shipments and keep the operation running "efficiently" and cannot afford to maintain a computer resource or process file that they rarely use or need.

Action Item 6.3

Find a copy of the most recent shop load analysis for your plant. Select the ten resources that show the maximum load.
- Review these resources and their loads with the shop supervisors.
- How many of these resources no longer run the parts that make up the load?
- How many are not even in the factory today?
- How many have not worked overtime in the last few months?
- How many of them are currently waiting for work?

Data inaccuracy is just one manifestation of the imperfection of the real world of manufacturing. The theory and the practical application of Synchronous Manufacturing will have to be developed with the explicit recognition of the reality of imperfection. Otherwise, like many other "looks good in theory" ideas, Synchronous Manufacturing will fail to provide real bottom-line benefits. What makes Synchronous Manufacturing a powerful technique is that it includes procedures for dealing with such real-life issues. It shows how best to apply the theory to real-world operations in a manner that will help reap most of the benefits. It does not require that the real world be modified to meet the requirements of the theory.

Action Item 6.4

- Estimate the time and effort it would take to clean up the basic information in your operation.
- How much of the data itself will have changed during this time?
- Do you think it will ever be totally accurate?

If the Bottleneck cannot be identified by using the data available in computer files, then how else can it be identified? What is offered in *The Goal,* for this purpose, is a specific application of the practical techniques of Synchronous Manufacturing. The application is to find the Bottlenecks in the Bearington plant. The technique is to use the scientific method of "cause and effect". Most plants are operated without the explicit recognition of Bottlenecks and the fundamentally different role they play. Most plants also operate under the traditional cost system. These "causes" will result in certain "effects" based on the nature of the operation. At the Bearington plant, these "effects" were the accumulation of inventories in specific areas (in front of the Bottlenecks) and a list of parts that always need to be expedited. If the relationship between the "cause" and the "effect" are known, then the procedure can be reversed and the "effect" can be used to identify the Bottleneck. This is how the Bearington plant managers identified the NCX-10 and Heat Treat as the Bottlenecks in their plant. The rest of the resources were Non-Bottlenecks.

Action Item 6.5

Consider the Constraint you "guessed" in Action item 6.1
- Predict some of the "effects" you expect if this is a Constraint.
- Verify that these effects actually exist in your plant.

A Comprehensive Approach

The general theory of how to predict the "effects" in any manufacturing plant is an integral part of Synchronous Manufacturing. It is comprehensive and systematic. Every manufacturing operation can be classified, based on the nature of its resource-product interactions, into one of three major classes:

1. V - Type Plant.
2. A - Type Plant.
3. T - Type Plant.

Depending on the nature of the product flow, all manufacturing operations fall into one of the three classes or represent a combination of them. The classification of manufacturing operations into these three types, based on the nature of the interactions, was originally done by Dr. Eliyahu M. Goldratt.

V - Type Plant

V-type plants are those manufacturing operations which have the following characteristics:

1. There are a few raw materials that result in a large number of end items.
2. All of the products are produced in essentially the same way.
3. Most V-Plants are capital intensive with specialized equipment.

Examples of plants that generally fall into this category are Textiles, Metals, Chemicals and others in the process and semi-process industries. Clearly, the technology and the market for textiles and for steel are very different. Nevertheless, most textile and steel plants will carry large finished goods inventories. This is because the traditional management practices and the specific nature of the re-source - product interactions are the same in both industries.

A - Type Plant

A-type plants are those manufacturing operations which have the following characteristics:

1. The assembly of parts that are manufactured by the same company is a dominant trait.
2. The manufactured parts are fairly unique to specific end products.

It also turns out that in A-Plants the parts share general-purpose machinery. Also, the different manufactured parts have dissimilar routings, in contrast to V-Plants where all the products have similar routings. Examples of A-Plants are those involved in major assemblies such as Aircraft Engines, Specialized Equipment, etc. Again, with widely differing markets and technologies, most A-type plants share a host of similar problems. Typical of the problems they experience are low resource utilizations, high unplanned overtime and a feeling that the Bottlenecks wander all the time. The reason for these common problems is the common management techniques they all employ.

T - Type Plant

T-type plants are those manufacturing operations which have the following characteristics:

1. Manufactured and purchased parts are common to many assemblies.
2. Each Assembly is made up of several common components.

The major difference with an A-Plant is the fact that component parts are common to the different assemblies. Examples of T-Plants are those involved in small appliances, electronic and electrical connectors, door locks, etc. Most of these suffer from an inability to provide good customer service. They also tend to carry very large finished goods and component parts inventories. Again, we have a case of common management techniques resulting in common problems, even though the plants are in diverse industries and markets.

The rules of Synchronous Manufacturing, developed in the next few chapters of this book, will help you to understand the "effects" of current management practices. This can then be reversed to identify the constraints in the plant. For example, in V-Plants the Bottlenecks can be identified from an analysis of the inventory profiles (the quantity and location of the in-process and finished goods inventories).

The classification of manufacturing facilities into V, A and T Plants and the systematic procedures for managing them requires more discussion than we can give it here (See Srikanth [9]). However, it is a basic concept of Synchronous Manufacturing.

7

*From Knowledge To Action**

T he Bottlenecks were identified at Bearington and their signifi-
cance to the plant had been recognized.

Bottlenecks control the Throughput of the plant.

Since Throughput (or on-time delivery) was a major problem in
the Bearington plant, it was clear that production at these resources
had to be improved. But how?

What happened when they tried to apply the new concepts Alex
had learned? As with any new concept, translating an understanding
of the ideas into practical application is far from trivial. Whenever
they tried to apply the concepts, they kept slipping back to the old
mode of thought and had great difficulty in implementing the concepts.
This difficulty lasted until the concepts were internalized through:

- Further understanding of the concepts and some guidelines for
  their use - this took place at the time of Jonah's visit.
- Application - as the Bearington plant tries here.
- Motivation - in this case, the imminent and obvious threat of
  Plant closure.
- Feedback - the results, as we will see.

*This chapter follows Chapters 19 - 21 of The Goal.[1] See Appendix A-7 for a
narrative summary of these chapters.*

The Bearington plant provides a textbook example of the implementation of these new concepts. It was not clear to the personnel how they could produce more at these Bottleneck resources. At first glance, it is easy to sympathize with their situation. After all, the Bottleneck is one area where the current focus on maximum efficiency and maximum production makes sense. So how can more production be achieved? The answer to this question came only after the people at the plant understood:

- The difference between Production and Throughput.
- The true value of a Bottleneck in bottom-line terms.

Additional investment is certainly one way to increase the capacity of the Bottleneck. However, if we are willing to change the way we manage these resources there are other less expensive ways to obtain the extra capacity. The goal is not to produce more pieces, but rather to increase Throughput, i.e. products that have been sold. To increase Throughput without producing more pieces, it is necessary to make sure that all of the pieces being produced are in fact needed for Throughput and not to fill a future order (i.e. for Inventory). Once the Bearington plant began to take these actions, the past due orders decreased at a very fast rate and customer satisfaction improved dramatically.

With hindsight, it seems obvious. But it is obvious only when relating the production at the resource, the Bottleneck, to the *operation as a whole* - the Throughput. As long as the production at a resource is looked at in isolation this is far from obvious. In fact, the visits from the expediters, who are trying to achieve Throughput by shipping products, are viewed as a nuisance and a disruption to the "normal business" of producing products efficiently.

The True Value Of A Bottleneck

Most resources in most manufacturing facilities have some hidden capacity that is not being utilized. The reason for this is that the "cost" of finding and utilizing this capacity exceeds the savings. In many cases there may be an expense to free up some capacity at a given resource. The cost of this capacity is calculated traditionally the same way whether or not the resource is a Bottleneck. Herein lies the fallacy of the traditional argument. The value of a resource to the entire operation is not simply the direct costs associated with that resource. The value of a resource depends upon its contribution to the T, I and OE of the plant. Since the Bottleneck controls the Throughput of the plant, its value is the selling price of the products that require its capacity. [1] (pp. 157)

A Synchronous Manufacturing Rule

A Bottleneck hour is equal to a system hour.

The value of the Bottleneck hour in the case of the Bearington plant turned out to be $2,735 (Annual sales of this product / Hours available per year).

Action Item 7.1

> - What is the current standard cost of one hour at a Bottleneck in your plant ?
> - What is the value of that hour ?

The true value of a Bottleneck resource completely changes the way trade-offs are viewed when searching for hidden capacity at this resource. Suddenly costs become easily justifiable when incurred in obtaining additional capacity at the Bottleneck. An excellent example of this is the decision by the Bearington management not to use an outside vendor for Heat Treat. When the cost charged by the outside vendor was compared with the standard cost of the same operation done in the Bearington plant, the cost charged by the outside vendor appeared excessive. As in the case of the Robot, the conventional approach based on incorrect assumptions, had resulted in decisions that were causing the plant to lose money.

Action Item 7.2

Consider a product that is processed at the Bottleneck work center in your plant:
- What is the "cost" of buying the completed part from an outside source?
- What is the standard cost of the same part?
- What is the true cost using the value of a Bottleneck hour?

Practical Ways
To More
Throughput

The utilization of a Bottleneck can be increased in a number of different ways. Four ways that Jonah discussed for consideration at Bearington were:[1] (pp. 151 - 159)

1. Make sure the Bottleneck never sits idle. This can be accomplished in many environments, such as the one at Bearington, by overlapping shifts and scheduling fill-in operators for lunches and other breaks.

2. Run only what is necessary for immediate and firm orders. Since production is not Throughput until it is sold, producing parts to maintain arbitrary efficiencies will steal from current Throughput.

3. Off-load Bottlenecks whenever possible. Each additional part produced is an additional unit sold. Thus, this makes sense even if standard costs and efficiencies indicate otherwise.

4. Strategically locate Quality Control points so that Bottlenecks are not running parts that should have been scrapped. This will eliminate wasting Bottleneck time on parts that will not contribute to the Throughput.

Action Item 7.3

- How many of these actions can be implemented in your plant?
- How many have already been implemented?
- What other ways can you improve the Throughput in your operation?
- What are some of the reasons for not having done them until now?

Moving To Action

Logically, the Bearington management was convinced they should begin to find ways to implement the above ideas. The hesitation on the part of some reflects the gap between intellectual recognition and movement to action. To move from knowledge to behavior requires that the concepts be internalized and that some guidelines be provided to facilitate initial action. Until the general concept of Throughput and the value of the "Bottleneck Hour" were explicitly demonstrated they were reluctant to act. And even then they needed some guidelines to follow.

In addition, a strong motivation factor has to be present. In the case of Bearington the threat was imminent. In other cases, the threat may not be as severe. But in today's global market few are immune to competitive threats, particularly from foreign manufacturers. When the threat is less imminent, the burden for creating the driving force and the leadership falls on the executives of the company. Without demonstrated leadership, the transition from knowledge and understanding to action and behavior will not take place. Without action benefits cannot be realized. Synchronous Manufacturing will remain only a technology that holds promise.

The new management decisions based on Synchronous Manufacturing must be converted to specific actions. In this attempt we again find several features of real-life manufacturing operations.

1. Clearly defined procedures must be developed in line with the new concepts. Developing a priority list for the parts that are processed by the Bottlenecks and instructing the operators to run strictly according to this list are examples.

2. In real life, things rarely go exactly according to plan. The first-line supervisors need guidelines for such eventualities. Without an understanding of the rationale for the new procedure, Bottlenecks at the Bearington plant were left idle. What should be done when the material, tooling, operator, etc. are not there when needed?

3. Interactions dominate life in manufacturing, even though most conventional techniques fail to recognize this. It is not possible to successfully operate the Bottleneck on a new policy, if the other resources (or at least those involved with these products) continue along the old lines. Not only the Bottleneck areas but the related areas should understand the why and the how of the new policies. The effect of focussing only on the Bottlenecks is discussed in the next chapter of this book.

Action Item 7.4

Focussing attention on the Bottleneck has the potential to increase the Throughput of your entire operation.
- What is the impact of a five percent increase of Throughput in your plant, with no increase in the workforce? (Refer to Chapter 3 for details of the calculation).

Adopting
A Competitive Strategy

The solution to becoming competitive does not lie in simply identifying the constraints and managing them differently. As discussed in Chapter Eight, this approach worked for a short while at Bearington, where making deliveries on time was a major business issue and constraints directly affected the Throughput of the plant. However, a total focus on constraints and complete neglect of the rest of the plant caused new problems to emerge quickly. In Chapter Nine we develop the full solution. Management policies are developed for all of the resources that are consistent with the overall goal of the business. The implementation of these policies requires the modification of some deep-seated concepts regarding the utilization of labor. Chapter Ten takes these discussions one final step, discussing an approach to the development of a competitive manufacturing strategy and the policies and procedures that are consistent with this strategy .

8

*Immediate Results But Complications Remain**

$\mathbf{S}$ ynchronous Manufacturing can help to identify the constraints of any business. As discussed in Chapter Six, these constraints may be physical elements, logistical elements, managerial elements or behavioral elements. Synchronous Manufacturing helps develop ways of managing the constraints so as to improve the performance of the company. As a result of this focussed approach, the benefits are realized very quickly. Within a week after the new policies for managing the two Bottlenecks (the NCX-10 and Heat Treat) went into effect at the Bearington facility, the results were already visible. The benefits essentially fell into two categories:

1. Hard bottom-line benefits as seen in reduced past-due orders.
2. A resurgence in meaningful Employee Involvement, as each employee began to focus on the global goal.

*Shipments Are Up--
Customers Are Happy*   Since the focus of the effort until then had been the Bottlenecks, which played a major role on the Throughput, the impact on the past due orders was immediate. In fact, the problem with deliveries was the most important business issue facing Bearington (remember Mr. Bill Peach's visit). The Bottlenecks were identified as the constraint to improving deliveries. Policies were established to maximize the

---

This chapter follows chapters 22 - 24 of The Goal.[1] See Appendix A-8 for a narrative summary of these chapters.

73

utilization of the Bottlenecks, resulting in an immediate impact on shipments. This process of identifying the constraint to improve major business issues is an essential part of Synchronous Manufacturing and, as previously stated, is done systematically. Managing the constraint in such a way as to have maximum impact on the total operation is another essential feature. Focussing on the right constraint and managing it properly will provide immediate and significant benefits.

Action Item 8.1

From the major programs you analyzed in Action Item 4.1, select one which was very successful and one not so successful as measured by T, I and OE.
- What is the connection between the activities planned under these two programs and the key business issue as stated in T, I and OE?

There is an acceleration in the rate of improvement as each employee begins to focus his effort toward the common goal. At the Bearington plant, this was seen in several instances:

1. The Quality Control Manager, Elroy Langston, and the Employee Relations Manager, Barbara Penn, made a recommendation that the parts that had been processed through the Bottlenecks be tagged so as to highlight their importance and immediately communicate this to all employees.

2. Bob Donovan, the seasoned Production Manager who had been the main voice of resistance to the new ideas until now, finally understood the logic of Alex Rogo's new approach. He aggressively searched for the "old" Zmegma machines to off-load some of the work from the Bottleneck machine, NCX-10.

This would have been inconceivable just a short while before, since such an action would have increased the unit cost of the products being off-loaded.

3. Ralph Nakamura, the Data Processing Manager, uncovered the fact that the Heat Treat operations were not manned all the time. In an attempt to achieve good utilization of available manpower (something all of us in manufacturing seek) the operators who loaded and unloaded the furnace were assigned to other Non-Bottleneck work centers while the furnace was in the heat treat cycle. When the cycle was finished, the furnace would wait until operators were "freed" from these other assignments. By seeking to achieve good utilization of the labor force, the Bottleneck was allowed to sit idle. With some difficulty, Alex Rogo convinced Bob Donovan to have operators on duty at Heat Treat at all times. No Bottleneck time was wasted, even though it appeared to be an inefficient action.

4. Mike Haley, the second shift Supervisor of the Heat Treat area, developed a method of loading the furnace that followed the sequence of the priority list and still managed to utilize the capacity of the furnace effectively. Since the furnace was a "Batch Processing" machine, this was not a simple task. Mike also developed a technique for reducing the furnace change-over time from an hour to a few minutes. This made more time available to the Bottleneck to process products. This translated to increased Throughput for the plant as a whole.

The interesting feature of each of these recommendations is that they are fairly simple to implement and cost very little money. However, none of these recommendations would have been conceived without a change in the focus of the employee. If the focus of management is on local measurements, then these will also be the focus of the employee. In such a case avenues to new ideas will remain closed. It is only when the employees begin to understand what they have to do in their local areas, to impact the entire operation, that such recommendations begin to flow.

Action Item 8.2

Consider some of the "support" functions in your operations, such as maintenance and Data Processing.
  • Select some specific activities and relate the activities of these functions to the common goal of T, I and OE.

Action Item 8.3

Successful Employee Involvement Programs must be more than pep rallies. They must relate what the individual employee is asked to do regarding the overall company and its objectives.
  • How is the Employee Involvement Program in your company accomplishing this and how successful is it?

The Benefits Hit
The Bottom Line
      The end of the month brought more good news to judge the efforts of Bottleneck management at Bearington. Of course, the results had to be judged on the operational measurements of T, I and OE. Shipments were at an all-time high. They were almost fifty percent higher than any other month in the history of the company. That meant Throughput was up. Work-in-process was down twelve percent from the previous month, so Inventory was down. Since Inventory was down and no labor had been added it is reasonable to assume that Operating Expense was down as well. The Bearington plant was making money and seemingly under control.

Bottlenecks Are Not
The Whole Answer

Every action that had been taken so far was focussed on the global goal of improving Bearington's customer service. Instead of looking internally and at each operation in isolation, the new approach of Synchronous Manufacturing focussed on improving the overall plant performance as seen by the customer. The focus was on Throughput and on Bottleneck parts. These were the most important.

In the analysis of the traditional cost system, we saw its most serious failing was that it ignored the resource-product interactions in manufacturing operations. At Bearington, they focussed exclusively on the Bottleneck and ignored the rest of the products and resources. But the interactions in manufacturing are too extensive to ignore the other parts and resources as Bearington had done. They paid the price immediately as parts not going through the Bottlenecks arrived late at assembly and shipments were affected. It appeared that they had successfully *shifted* the problem. To achieve a sound and lasting fix to their Throughput problems, they had to understand more than how to manage the Bottlenecks. They had to understand how to manage the rest of the plant as well.

9

*Order On The Factory Floor At Last**

T he Bearington plant managers focussed all their attention on the Bottlenecks and virtually ignored the rest of the plant. Suddenly they realized that new problems were emerging everywhere and threatened to negate the progress they felt they had made. The reason they ran into this difficulty is that while they had changed the policy by which they ran the Bottlenecks, they continued to run the Non-Bottleneck machines as before. The only change in policy here was to focus on producing the Bottleneck parts at the expense of parts that did not go through the Bottleneck. This quickly created a situation in which Non-Bottleneck parts were being ignored altogether. Since there was a stock of these parts ahead of the assembly operation they could maintain shipments for a short while. When this stock of parts was depleted the products could not be assembled. This time it was not due to lack of Bottleneck parts but due to the lack of Non-Bottleneck parts.

In the Bearington plant there were only two Bottleneck resources. The majority of resources were Non-Bottlenecks. In most cases the number of resources that are Bottlenecks is very few. In many cases, there may not be any Bottlenecks at all. Therefore, it is important that appropriate policies be established for these resources as well. A plant in which the majority of resources are operating on incorrect policies cannot be expected to remain productive for long.

This chapter follows chapters 25 & 26 of The Goal.[1] See Appendix A-9 for a narrative summary of these chapters.

What is the appropriate policy for managing Non-Bottleneck resources? To answer this question we must understand how Bottlenecks and Non-Bottlenecks interact in our plants and how they affect the overall measures of T, I and OE. If we look at Bottleneck and Non-Bottleneck resources, it is the flow of material that creates interactions between the resources. Consider the case where the material is processed first at the Bottleneck resource (X) and then by the Non-Bottleneck resource (Y).

Clearly, in this case the ability of Y to produce product is controlled by what is processed by X. This can be summarized by the rule :[1] (pp. 209)

A Synchronous Manufacturing Rule

The utilization of a Non-Bottleneck resource is controlled by the constraints of the system.

Consider the case where the material is first processed at a Non-Bottleneck resource and then by the Bottleneck resource:

There is nothing to prevent the Y resource from producing at its own pace, which by definition is faster than that of X. While this is possible, it serves no useful purpose. The X resource still controls the Throughput of the system, since it has to process the product before it can be sold. Thus, if Y is operated at its own pace it will increase Inventory and will not contribute to the Throughput of the plant. This can be summarized by the rule:[1] (pp. 210)

Activation and Utilization are not the same.

Action Item 9.1

> Play the Production Dice Game (Appendix B) with unbalanced resources. Identify the regions of the Dice Game that represent the two flow patterns discussed above.
> * Review the results including the overall team performance (T, I, and OE) and the performance of each resource (utilization).
> * How do these results afford proof of the above rules?

At this point it appears that the only harm of over-activation is the build up of Inventory. We saw the build up of Inventory at the Bearington plant. Since Throughput, particularly delivery to promises, was their major problem this would not appear to be an overriding concern. However, the harm of over-activation is far more serious than just a build up of Inventory. To see this we must consider resource interactions that are slightly more complex than the basic building blocks discussed above. We will define resource interaction as follows:

Resource Interaction   **Two resources interact with each other when activity at one resource can influence the activity or the result of the activity at the other resource.**

In this sense, resources interact in three ways:

1. There is a direct flow of material, as discussed above.
2. The interaction is created by the fact that the products from the two resources are both required to assemble the final product that is sold. There is no direct flow of product from one

resource to the other. An example of this is shown below, and was discussed by Jonah.

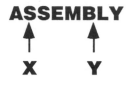

We can see that in this case the rules still hold and the consequence of over-activation is excess Inventory. If the Y resource produces more than needed to keep pace with production by the X resource, then these parts will accumulate in front of the assembly operation. They cannot be converted to Throughput since the mating parts are not available. They may appear as useful production for the departments or feeder plants that produce them, but for the business as a whole it is Inventory and not Throughput. This was precisely the case of the Bearington Plant Robot.

3. When resources work on multiple products, as most resources do, then what one resource does on one product influences what other resources can and should do on other products. An example of this is the following situation which existed at the Bearington facility. The milling machine was a Non-Bottleneck machine. It produced several parts. Some of these parts were processed at a later stage by the Bottleneck machine NCX-10 and others were not. The following diagram shows the representative case with one of each type. When the milling machine was "over-activated" on the Bottleneck parts it caused two things to happen simultaneously:

MILLING MACHINE ⟶ NCX-10

MILLING MACHINE ⟶ Other Resources Only

Firstly, since the rate of production at the milling machine was greater than at the NCX-10, there was a buildup of Inventory of these parts in front of the NCX-10.

Secondly, the over-activation was done at the expense of the parts that did not involve the NCX-10. This caused the shortage of these parts at Assembly and created the impression that "new Bottlenecks" were emerging. Parts shortage at assembly meant that products could not be shipped, and therefore Throughput was lost.

The consequence of over-activation can thus be far more serious than a buildup of Inventory. It can result in a loss of Throughput. It is more important in this case to understand that Activation is not the same as Utilization. The priority system that was implemented at Bearington caused precisely this type of over-activation and of course the results were exactly what can be anticipated. The scientific method of cause and effect is at work again.

Action Item 9.2

> • Analyze the flow of material in your plant and identify examples of the three types of interactions.

While the effects of over-activation are very serious, current management procedures actually encourage over-activation while discouraging under-activation.

Action Item 9.3

> Analyze the way in which shop supervisors are evaluated in your company.
> - How do these measures encourage over-activation?

It should be clear from the discussion involving the three types of resource-product interactions, that the effects of over-activation in particular, and of the traditional management philosophy in general, will depend on the nature of the resource interactions that exist in the plant and on which particular interaction is dominant.

Action Item 9.4

> - In those cases discussed in Action Item 9.2, what should be the consequences of over-activation?
> - Do you see these "effects" in your plant today?

Interactions-
The Key To Control
What are the consequences of over-activation? The answer will depend on the type of resource-product interactions that are present. In the discussion above we analyzed at some length some of the basic interactions and the effects of over-activation in each case. It is possible to make a list of all possible resource-product interactions. If we do this we will find that there are twelve basic interactions we must deal with. The effects of over-activation in each case can be quite easily determined.

A complex plant has many different resources and many different products. Within the plant, several of the interactions discussed here will be present simultaneously. To really understand the plant, we must understand the effect of the combination of these basic interactions. In our experience, there are three combinations of the twelve major interactions that are the most common. The corresponding plants are referred to as V-Plants, A-Plants and T-Plants. All manufacturing plants will fall into one of these three categories. If we understand the type of plant we can predict the "effects" of traditional management techniques - the "effects" of policies that:

- Try to balance the capacity of the plant.
- Fail to recognize the difference between Bottlenecks and Non-Bottlenecks.
- Tend to over-activate all resources.

A V-Plant managed according to these policies will manifest the characteristic of having large finished goods inventories. This was one of the common issues that V-Plants shared as discussed in Chapter Three.

We can begin to understand why manufacturing operations behave the way they do! It is not because they are too complex, too uncertain or too hostile. It is because of the fundamental nature of the production process and the way it has been managed; the way all of us in America have managed our operations.

From this understanding of the specific causes of specific problems, specific solutions can be developed in a systematic fashion. And as in the case of Bearington, the solutions can be implemented in a definite sequence to achieve a rapid, controlled and sustained improvement.

Managing Non-Bottlenecks

So what is the appropriate policy for managing Non-Bottleneck resources? Clearly, the current policy that encourages over-activation must be replaced. The priority scheme that Bearington was using at this point was a variation of this same basic policy. They were over-activating Bottleneck parts and neglecting the other parts. Once the full damage caused by over-activation is realized, the policy for Non-Bottlenecks is almost self-evident.

> **Non-Bottlenecks should only be activated to support the Throughput of the plant.**

Since this is controlled by the Bottlenecks, Non-Bottlenecks should keep pace with Bottlenecks. They should not produce more than required and they should not produce earlier than required.

> **Non-Bottlenecks should produce only <u>what</u> is needed, <u>when</u> it is needed!**

This is a deceptively simple-sounding policy that is far from easy to implement. Once more, the obstacle is the traditional system. If a Non-Bottleneck only produces what is needed, and by definition it takes less time to do so than the Bottleneck, the Non-Bottleneck should not be working all the time. Since the majority of resources, including a majority of the labor force, is in the Non-Bottleneck category, the above "obvious" management policy will imply that:

> **The majority of the resources should not be working all the time!!!**

This deceptively simple rule poses a monumental policy barrier and a monumental psychological barrier when we try to implement it.

The Policy Barrier   The monumental policy barrier is that if resources (labor, in particular) are not working on products, then variances will increase and this will escalate the cost of the product. It does not matter to the cost system that the product is not needed and will only end up as inventory. The managers at Bearington recognized this fact immediately, as all manufacturing managers would. They decided to postpone dealing with the ramifications at the division office and proceeded with implementing the new "obvious" policy. This was discovered fairly quickly and the Bearington managers were reprimanded. It is therefore of prime importance that senior executives and financial managers be educated as to the manner in which the traditional cost system will evaluate the new actions. Without the concurrence of these executives, the magnitude of benefits that can be realized will be limited and the chances for success are marginal.

Action Item 9.5

> Identify some of the policies currently in force in your operations that would present an obstacle to implementing such a policy of not over-activating. Some examples are discussed in the paragraph below.

The Psychological Barrier   The monumental psychological barrier is the result of many years of working with the traditional system. Can we accept that most of the workers in our plant will not be working all of the time? This is the point at which one might begin to feel that--

"In our plant, most labor is in the Bottleneck category".

Perhaps rereading Chapter Five of this book will convince you that this is most likely not the case in your plant.

The current system for evaluating shop supervisors will present a barrier to the implementation of this "Just-In-Time" policy. Incentive schemes present similar barriers. The entire financial and labor reporting systems as used in most companies are designed not only to pick up "idle" worker time to fractional time units but also to classify and categorize these "inefficiencies" so they can be "rectified" by the responsible managers. What we have here is indisputable logic facing an overwhelming barrier. In the Bearington plant, for example, we saw the shop manager, Bob Donovan, repeatedly objecting to such policies.

The KANBAN system of production used in many Japanese companies is an example of a system in which not all of the workers are working all of the time. The traditional system would consider such a system as inefficient. The tremendous success of the Japanese companies using this approach has finally forced us to admit that it is very effective. Many American companies acknowledge it as superior to systems in America and are trying to implement it in their plants. Since many of these attempts lack the explicit recognition of this conflict between the traditional cost system and KANBAN, the overall success rate of such attempts in America has not been good.

Because the feeling that "idle time" is unproductive is so deeply rooted, it is necessary to clarify the recommendation for managing Non-Bottleneck resources. This is not to say that excess idle time or excess capacity is desirable. The argument is that it is better to acknowledge the existence of excess capacity (a certain amount of which is unavoidable) and tolerate the resulting idle time, than it is to use the excess capacity to create inventory. If this is done, the idle time becomes available for use in other ways. Hence, we prefer to call the idle time (once it is exposed) *opportunity time*. It represents an amount of time we now have available at most resources that we can utilize productively (as measured by T, I and OE).

How can we productively utilize this opportunity? We will see in the next chapter how the Bearington plant took advantage of this opportunity time to improve their competitive position in the marketplace. The key to successful management of this time is to identify tasks that can be performed during the available time that will benefit the company as a whole. For example, if a Non-Bottleneck work center completes its allocated work and there is still time left before the next task can be started, then we can use the time of this resource to assist the Bottleneck work center in whatever ways possible. Non-Bottlenecks which have excess time available can be utilized to assist other Non-Bottlenecks which have seriously fallen behind schedule. The opportunity time can be used to practice setups, undergo cross training, attend quality circles or other activities that will help the resource perform its work more effectively.

Action Item 9.6

Consider some of the resources in your plant that are Non-Bottlenecks (particularly labor).
- Generate a list of activities that can be performed by these resources to utilize their opportunity time.
- Compare the impact of these activities on T, I and OE with the negative impact of converting this time into Inventory.

The one thing that should not be done with this opportunity time is to use it for essential and planned activities. If a resource is required to perform a task, then of course the time required to perform this task must be excluded from the available opportunity time. Attempting to fill idle time with necessary and planned work is simply an attempt to balance the capacity of the resource. We have already determined that this is neither possible nor desirable.

The DBR System   In the Bearington plant, the concepts discussed above were immediately implemented to synchronize the production process to the true capabilities of the plant, represented by the Bottlenecks. The system used to control the production process is called the Drum-Buffer-Rope system or the DBR system. The terminology "DBR System" for such an approach to material control systems was introduced by Goldratt and Fox. [7] (pp. 98 - 114)

The Bottleneck is the drum.

It controls the Throughput of the plant and sets the "pace" of production.

Release of material should be tied to the capabilities of the Bottleneck. Bottleneck parts should be released only at the rate that they will be processed by the Bottleneck resource. Too much will only build inventory and too little will starve the Bottleneck. Non-Bottleneck parts should be released at the rate at which they will be consumed at the Assembly operation. Too much will build inventory and too little will cause shortages at Assembly and missed deliveries.

The tying of material release to the pace of the drummer is analogous to using a Rope .

The Bottleneck should be protected from unexpected problems at the feeder Non-Bottleneck resources. This can be done by planning to have material queued up a small time before it is needed.

Such an inventory buffer is called a Time Buffer.

The Time Buffer is not to be confused with the random piles of materials that are found on the shop floor today. Time Buffers are located in very few spots and have precisely defined content. They should contain the work that will be performed by the work center that is buffered in the immediate future. Also, in accordance with this definition, as the schedule for the buffered work center changes, the content of the Time Buffer will change. It is worthwhile emphasizing that most work centers, which will be in the Non-Bottleneck category, will not be buffered at all.

Action Item 9.7

Select two work centers in your operation - one of which is a suspected Bottleneck. Identify the work-in-process queue in front of each resource.
  • Using the "schedule" for these resources, draw a graph showing the hours of work this in-process queue represents for each day. (Count work scheduled for today and all past due as due today - day zero).
  • What should the time buffer in front of a known Non-Bottleneck look like?

To establish a DBR system we must begin by establishing:

  • The drum and its operating policies.
  • The exact location and size of the buffers.
  • The policies for operating Non-Bottleneck resources.

This gives us the production plan, which when executed will give us the best deliveries with the lowest Inventories and Operating Expense consistent with the policies and constraints established. Of course, when we try to execute the plan, things will not always go smoothly. Procedures for dealing with these disruptions must also be established.   Otherwise, as we saw in Chapter Seven, where the Bottleneck was allowed to stand idle, the full benefits from the DBR system will not be realized. Thus in addition to the DBR system, we must establish:

  • The policies for dealing with the everyday problems on the shop floor.

The methodology essentially depends on the type of plant one has, whether V, A or T . The type of plant and the specific needs of the business can be used to establish detailed procedures for achieving a smooth flow of material through the factory.   Successful implementation of a DBR system will result in a smooth and orderly production process, with reliable deliveries, very low inventories and a minimum of unplanned overtime. (For a complete discussion of the DBR system see Srikanth. [9])

Action Item 9.8

Set up a DBR system for the Production Dice Game (Appendix B) with unbalanced resources.

10
Manufacturing Becomes
A Competitive Weapon*

Synchronous Manufacturing recognizes that plant resources fall into two categories, Bottlenecks and Non-Bottlenecks. It helps identify the resources or elements that are the constraints of the business. It also helps establish the proper operating policies for Constraints as well as the Non-Constraints, recognizing the impact of these resources on T, I and OE. The material control system that is consistent with Synchronous Manufacturing concepts is the DBR system. Implementation of the DBR system of material control helps regain control of the production process. The table below summarizes the shop floor situation in the Bearington plant before and after the system was implemented.

Impact Of DBR System Implementation At Bearington

Before	After
1. Many past due orders.	No past due orders.
2. Delivery promises very unreliable	Delivery promises reliable to within a day.
3. Production lead time longer than four months.	Production lead time less than eight weeks.
4. Very high inventories.	Inventories shrinking rapidly.

*This chapter follows chapters 27 - 31 of The Goal. [1] See Appendix A-10 for a narrative summary of these chapters.

Before	**After**
5. High unplanned overtime.	No unplanned overtime.
6. Over 40% of shipments in the last week of month.	Shipments are uniform - 25% each week.
7. Production environment very chaotic - serious tension between functional groups.	Production environment under control and a spirit of cooperation between the groups.
8. Employees uninvolved and lackadaisical.	Employees involved and spirited.

Bearington Healthy But Unit Costs Go Up

At this stage, the Bearington plant was producing the products to satisfy their demand with less effort than before. Clearly, as a business, they were more profitable. However, like most companies that reach this point in the implementation, they were faced with two major problems:

1. A perceived problem with the division or corporate office.
2. A real problem sustaining improvements.

The perceived problem with the division or corporate office. In implementing the DBR system and using the concept of Utilization and Activation they had explicitly recognized the existence of excess capacity. A resource with excess capacity has some excess time available. This is the time left over after that resource has produced all the products required to satisfy the production plan. This excess time is referred to as idle time, since the resource is idle (not producing) during this time. We prefer to call this time "Opportunity Time", since the excess capacity represents an element that can be exploited to our benefit. An example of how the Bearington plant exploited this opportunity time is discussed in the next section.

If the distinction between Activation and Utilization is understood, then all resources will not be managed in such a way as to achieve full activation. This is how synchronization is achieved, and both the inventory and the production lead time are significantly reduced. In the early phase of the implementation, when inventory levels drop rapidly, this idle time is at its maximum and is most visible. The problem with division or corporate management will precipitate because this non-production time will show up as a decrease in the operating efficiency or as an increase in the unit cost of the product (labor variance or unabsorbed burden).

Action Item 10.1

In your operation, select some departments that you are certain are Non-Bottlenecks.
- How would an increase in "idle" or "unutilized" time of 5% show up in the unit costs of the products produced in this department?
- How would they affect the evaluation of the entire operation?

In an attempt to hold off the inevitable, the Bearington plant tried to avoid this problem by making "unauthorized" changes to the cost base. It would have been better to involve the corporate managers from the outset. Then, they would have known what to expect and would have understood why the "numbers" did not tell the full story.

It is also important to recognize this apparent inefficiency is not a real problem for the business as a whole. Since more product is produced with the same resources and with less total expense (less inventory, less overtime, less freight, etc.) the business as a whole is more profitable. This is true even though the manufacturing operation in the transition phase appears less efficient. If the operation managers are measured by the conventional yardsticks of operating efficiency and unit cost then for them, this is a real problem.

A real problem of sustaining the improvements. When implementing the DBR system and when improving the productivity of the Bottleneck resources, the ability of the plant to move more product out the door is enhanced. This was seen at Bearington, where they completely eliminated past-due orders. Without any increase in plant capacity, they produced enough to meet current demand and eliminate all past-due orders. As a result, the Throughput of the plant was very high during this period. This showed in the extremely positive monthly report card from Bearington.

However, there was a problem once the past-due orders were eliminated. The ability to produce more still existed, but it could not be converted into Throughput. Without the additional demand the production would end up as Finished Goods Inventory. The only way to sustain the level of profitability was to create demand. Bill Peach decreed the demise of the Bearington plant if the level of improvement could not be sustained. The only real solution that Alex Rogo could think of was to increase sales.

Action Item 10.2

An alternative to increasing sales is to try to produce the current demand with perhaps fewer resources.
- Compare the difference in profitability for your operation between selling more products with the same resources and trying to reduce the resources to support current sales.

But how can sales be increased? This requires a clear understanding of the competitive factors in the specific marketplace.

Action Item 10.3

- What are the most significant competitive elements among Product, Price, Delivery and Quality?
- Which one of these can you impact quickly and most directly with your manufacturing operations? (Note that your competitors may answer this question differently.)

Once the management team has identified which competitive element to exploit, the problem should be attacked with a two-pronged approach, one spearheaded by the manufacturing faction and the other spearheaded by the sales and marketing faction.

1. The manufacturing managers should aggressively pursue improving the chosen competitive factor. For example, in Bearington's case the lead time quoted to a customer was selected as the competitive element to pursue. The manufacturing managers had seen for themselves the drop in lead time from four months to less than eight weeks. Not only were the lead times shorter, the reliability of their promises had increased significantly. With Jonah's help, they understood how they could reduce it even further (to three to four weeks) without affecting the reliability of their promises. Again, this was done by first understanding the cause for the current lead times.

2. The second element in realizing the Throughput potential is that the sales force should aggressively pursue new orders by leveraging this competitive element. At Bearington, the sales manager pursued new sales with the promise of quick and reliable deliveries. Since lead time was a major competitive factor in their marketplace (as in most) new orders were quickly generated.

How was the Lead Time reduced? The lead time is the time the product spends on the factory floor. For most of this time it is simply waiting for other parts required for assembly (wait time) or waiting for a resource to become available (queue time).

Action Item 10.4

> •   What is your current lead time?
> Select some of the major components/products and calculate the time the product spends being worked on. This is the sum of the process times and setup times of the operations required for that product.
> •   How does this actual production time compare with your current lead time?

By synchronizing the production process, much of the time the product spends idle on the factory floor is eliminated. To reduce the lead time even further, we have to reduce the batch size we use. Appendix C discusses the relationship between batch sizes and lead times in some detail.

The Importance Of Production Lead Times

Reducing the production lead time has benefits that go beyond a simple reduction of in-process inventories. The more we try to understand the reasons for the major successes of the Just-In-Time systems for managing production operations, the more it becomes clear that the successes are due to a zealous drive to reduce in-process inventories to an absolute minimum. In fact, the actions that are required to regain competitive position are also the actions that are required to operate the production process with lower inventories. Among the competitive factors that are directly related to reducing in-process inventories are: [7] (pp. 36 - 66).

1. The ability to introduce the new products to the market quickly.
2. The ability to identify the cause of quality problems.
3. The ability to improve the reliability of shipments to promises.
4. The ability to reduce the lead time from order receipt to shipment.
5. The ability to reduce operating costs by reducing costs associated with the above elements as well as inventory carrying costs.

In addition to improving the production operation, reducing lead times has another beneficial effect. It significantly reduces the level of finished goods inventories required and reduces the typical chaos on the factory floor caused by demand fluctuations. This is due to the fact that the accuracy of forecasts tends to deteriorate the farther out in time one is required to forecast. A typical curve of forecast accuracy is shown in the diagram below.

Figure 10.1

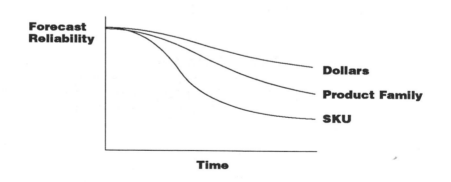

Note that the most serious deterioration occurs when looking at the forecast of individual items. But the production floor cannot work with averages. They have to work with specific products and hence, they are working with a curve which degrades very rapidly over time.

Before a company can begin production, the product demand must be forecasted. The longer the production lead time the further into the future one must look to predict product demand, and the more unreliable the prediction will be. Therefore, in terms of the actual demand, the product at the early stage of the production cycle is often the wrong one.

Once the problem is identified, a scramble begins to produce the appropriate product to meet actual demand. However, this must be accomplished in what is then less than the standard lead time, contributing to the unreliability of production lead times.

Compounding the problem further is the fact that unreliable forecasts and unreliable production lead times cause finished goods inventories to soar in an attempt to maintain customer service. The more competitive the market, the more volatile the demand in the respect that the customer has more options from which to choose, and the inventory becomes a bigger liability both in terms of direct costs and its impact on the competitive elements previously described. ("The Importance of Production Lead Times")

Action Item 10.5

> - Plot the graph of forecast reliability as a function of time for your business, using historical data - for the total dollar sales, by product family and by specific SKU.
> - What is the impact on the level of Finished Goods Inventory you have to carry to support your service level targets when the production lead time is cut in half?
> - Convert this impact on Inventory into financial terms.

Small Batches Smooth Flow

As the batch size is reduced, the number of setups will increase. Most resources are Non-Bottlenecks and have "excess" capacity available. This excess capacity can be used to perform the extra setups necessary. This is one example of how the "opportunity" time can be exploited properly. Excess capacity can be used (measured by the global measurements of T, I and OE) to gain a competitive advantage.

Also, as the Bearington plant discovered, when working with smaller batches, the material flows through the plant more smoothly. The work load at most work centers is uniform instead of the feast or famine scenario of before. The only remaining problem is the apparent increase in the cost of the product caused by the increased setups. We all recognize that if we are producing the same volume of product with the same number of operators, and doing so with far less inventory and in far less time; then we must be making more money, no matter what the numbers say. If the implementation program was done properly, the senior executives are aware of this and the apparent increase in production costs will not be an issue.

In just a short time, and without any expenditures to speak of, the Bearington plant management was able to promise their customer's deliveries in four weeks and keep that promise. This would have been considered inconceivable before implementing the new techniques.

Developing A Competitive Strategy

The important point here concerns the way in which the sales strategy is developed. A sales strategy is often devised at senior executive levels with very little consideration for the manufacturing function. This strategy is then thrust upon the manufacturing operations in the expectation that they adopt the goal as their own. In the approach used here, manufacturing becomes an integral factor in the strategic decision-making process.

Action Item 10.6

- What are the procedures your company uses in developing a business strategy?
- How is this business strategy converted to a manufacturing strategy?

This approach to developing a business strategy is in strong contrast to the traditional method used by most companies in America. The major elements of developing such a strategy are:

1. <u>Identifying the specific competitive elements and how they impact the business.</u> Is it price, delivery, quality or product? What does improvement in each of these areas mean to additional sales and market share? At the Bearington plant the priority of the competitive elements may be price, delivery, and quality.

2. <u>Understanding the specific resource-product interactions of the manufacturing operations.</u> This means understanding the nature of the Bearington plant, the relative location of the Bottlenecks in the product flow and the implications of different operating policies.

3. <u>Matching the manufacturing operation to the competitive elements and determine the business strategy.</u> This will mean identifying which competitive element has the best potential for improving the business performance and will take into account the expense of making the improvements and the potential gain in sales or reduction in plant operating expenses. The competitive element chosen at the Bearington plant was lead time to deliver the product. This could be achieved with a change in operating policies at no additional expense.

4. <u>Establishing the logistical and technical systems and procedures to realize both the improvements in the manufacturing process and the increase in sales.</u> The plant implemented the batch sizing decisions and the sales force searched for orders where the lead times were a factor.

5. <u>Repeating the process by redefining the business issues and the new</u>

competitive elements and considering the new manufacturing operations with the new policies and any new products and processes.

Action Item 10.7

> The reduction in lead time represents the second step in the process of improvement at Bearington. The first step was the improvement in customer deliveries.
> - Identify the discrete strategic steps in that first step.

The major difference with traditional approaches to developing business strategies is that the manufacturing operation is an integral factor in the development of the overall strategy. Market needs (the competitive factors) and the specific manufacturing capabilities are analyzed simultaneously to determine the most effective strategy for the specific business. The question being asked is:

What is the best way to compete in the marketplace with the specific manufacturing operation ?

In the terminology of Robert Hayes and Steven Wheelwright, the Bearington plant has reached a level IV status.[2]

Synchronous Manufacturing
An Overview

The management philosophy that helped achieve the rapid turnaround of the Bearington plant is called Synchronous Manufacturing. Chapter Eleven defines the key elements of this new philosophy. We also discuss how Synchronous Manufacturing helps focus managerial effort to those actions that are required to implement the manufacturing strategy. No single program applied across the board will solve our problems. Each of the new technologies must be employed only where they can further the overall strategy. Both the strategy itself and the constraints to the strategy must be continuously evaluated. The implementation of such a basic change raises several organizational issues. Chapter Twelve discusses the key elements required for the successful adoption of this (or any other) new philosophy. We also discuss the organizational responsibility for each element and the requirements of each of these elements. We conclude with a recap of the full power of Synchronous Manufacturing.

11
How Was It All Accomplished?

At the point in the story when the Bearington plant appears to have been resurrected, a number of startling gains have been achieved:

1. They gained a large order for ten thousand units based on their ability to deliver products quickly and reliably. Additional sales gains appeared to be very realistic, based on their new performance.

2. Inventories were reduced by sixty percent. This major reduction in inventory had not affected their ability to make shipments when promised. As illustrated in this book, the actions taken to reduce inventory were precisely what was needed to improve their delivery performance. High inventories had hindered, rather than helped them to achieve reliable deliveries.

3. The end-of-the-month syndrome (shipping almost forty percent of the monthly shipment in the last week of the month) was eliminated. This resulted in less overtime towards the end of the month and improved the flow of revenues to the business.

Thus, in a very short period of time, the plant increased Throughput significantly, while achieving major gains in Inventory and Operating Expense. They were making money.

This amazing turnaround was accomplished through the use of a new management technology called Synchronous Manufacturing. [1,6,7] Even after reading this book to this point or after reading *The Goal*[1], most managers have difficulty explaining this new technology precisely. They have difficulty with the question:

What is Synchronous Manufacturing?

Action Item 11.1

> Compare responses from the different people in your organization to the following question:
> * Exactly how was the turnaround at Bearington accomplished?

Synchronous Manufacturing

We have seen Synchronous Manufacturing applied at Bearington and we have understood the various aspects of Synchronous Manufacturing. But, we still have a difficult time describing it. The simplest and most succinct definition of Synchronous Manufacturing is the following:

Synchronous Manufacturing is a management philosophy in which every action is focussed on the common global goal.

This deceptively simple philosophy can achieve rapid improvements in most manufacturing businesses because it provides the means to define and focus on the common goal. To successfully implement such a philosophy, we need a way to define the common goal such that it is meaningful to everyone in the organization. We need a way to relate the individual actions to this common goal and we need a way of managing the various actions so as to achieve the greatest benefit. These are the three essential elements of Synchronous Manufacturing:

Three Major Elements

1. <u>Synchronous Manufacturing introduces a new set of operational measurements.</u> These are Throughput (T), Inventory (I), and Operating Expense (OE). The key features of these measures are that:

    a. They are intrinsic to the manufacturing operation.
    b. They are global measurements for the entire operation.

By shifting attention from local costs to these global measures, Synchronous Manufacturing makes it possible for each individual to relate to the common global goal.

2. <u>Synchronous Manufacturing provides a set of guiding rules or principles that enable us to relate specific actions to the operation as a whole.</u> This is necessary to effectively use the global measures of T, I, and OE. These rules were used in the Bearington plant, for example, to establish effective systems for:

    a. Evaluating alternate marketing and production strategies in terms of their impact on T, I and OE for the operation as a whole.

    b. Establishing the proper material and production control

system to achieve the best performance in terms of T, I and OE.

Action Item 11.2

> - Define Throughput, Inventory and Operating Expense.
> - State the rules of Synchronous Manufacturing.
> - How were these rules used in Bearington to:
>   1) Evaluate the "Make/Buy" decision at the heat treat operation?
>   2) Determine the cost of reducing batch sizes?

The activities undertaken at the Bearington plant were primarily production activities and hence, our discussions in this book have also focussed on production activities. However, the actions in a manufacturing organization include more than just production activities. All of these actions (whether they relate to Engineering, Purchasing, Data Processing, or any other activity) must be evaluated in terms of the impact on the global measures T, I and OE. Policies and systems for all of these activities must be established to achieve the best performance in terms of these measurements.

3. <u>Synchronous Manufacturing provides a set of systematic procedures that enable the above systems to be used in complex manufacturing operations</u>. These include procedures for:

   a. Classifying manufacturing operations into their type, V, A or T plants. This is done so that the effects of traditional management methods can be quickly identified and those policies and procedures most likely to be in conflict with improving competitiveness can be identified.

   b. Identifying the constraints, whether they are physical, managerial, logistical or behavioral.

   c. Focussing attention on the areas of the operation that offer the greatest leverage for global improvement.

Action Item 11.3

> • How was Synchronous Manufacturing used to identify the constraint in the following cases.
> 1) Ship the promised quantities on time.
> 2) Reduce the production lead times.

Again, the primary constraints in the Bearington plant were production constraints. In a general manufacturing operation this need not be the case. It may, for example, be a purchasing policy that is the constraint. It may be the proliferation of product design that is the primary constraint to effective operation. No matter what the constraint, it must be identified and addressed if the business is to achieve rapid improvement.

Focussing
The Improvements How did Synchronous Manufacturing help improve the Bearington plant? Synchronous Manufacturing did not introduce any new processes or machine technologies. Yet as a result of adopting Synchronous Manufacturing, Bearington was able to produce more products with the same resources as before and at the same time reduce inventories and manufacturing lead times significantly. How was this possible?

The answer to how Synchronous Manufacturing helps a manufacturing business lies in its ability to help management focus their efforts. It helps identify the constraint to improving the business, and it helps in asking the right questions when discussing the various aspects of the business. For example, at Bearington the question of how to produce more at the Bottlenecks was raised. At Non-Bottlenecks it raised a different question - how to reduce inventories and operating expenses by achieving a smooth material flow? Asking the right question is ninety percent of the solution to any problem. Once the appropriate question has been asked then the burden for actually achieving the result falls on the appropriate functional group in the company. Consider the problem of producing more at the Bottleneck. All of the various elements that take away from productive utilization of the Bottleneck were analyzed. This included, among other elements:

1. Time lost due to defective materials.
2. Lack of proper prioritization of the work in queue.

The first element is clearly a Quality Assurance matter. This department analyzed the situation and devised a way to identify most of the defects before the products were processed by the Bottlenecks. The second item was the responsibility of Material and Production Control. They worked with Data Processing to devise a way to better communicate the priority of each shop order to the Bottleneck work centers.

The above examples bring to light two important aspects of the application of Synchronous Manufacturing. First, it focussed the efforts of Quality Assurance and Material Control. Second, it provided them with a different system to evaluate the impact of their actions. Improvements of this type at the Bottleneck work centers improve the Throughput of the entire plant and hence their value is very high. A traditional cost-based analysis in all likelihood, would have led the Bearington managers to the conclusion that the additional costs of implementing these recommendations would not be justifiable, since the cost saving was very small. Thus Synchronous Manufacturing not only focusses the activities of the organization, it also provides a different yardstick for evaluating these activities.

Synchronous Manufacturing-- A Philosophy, Not A Technique

Synchronous Manufacturing is not a productivity program in the conventional sense. Consider for example, an Automation program. First a decision is made that automation is the most effective approach to the company's manufacturing problems. Then all of the processes in the plant are analyzed for automation opportunities. The value of automation at each process (where automation is possible) is calculated in the conventional way using reductions in direct labor, improvements in quality and reliability, etc. This analysis serves as the basis for determining which processes will be automated and in which sequence. In this analysis step, the connection between the strategic basis for choosing an automation program is lost. We are back to looking at operations in isolation and from a cost and efficiency viewpoint. From a strategic viewpoint (i.e. to achieve a desired result for the business as a whole) the best candidate for automation often has very little to do with direct cost savings. Thus the potential strategic benefits of automation are not realized when the program is implemented. The Robot at Bearington is an excellent example of how a powerful new technology can be misapplied. A Quality program, similarly, is designed to identify and correct quality problems at each operation. Again the analysis is usually done without considering the operation as a whole and the "potential benefits" are often not realized. The analysis in the previous section of the value of inspection before the Bottlenecks provides a good example.

Action Item 11.4

Consider some of the major programs that have been implemented in your company, such as MRP, SPC, Quality, Automation, etc.
- How were the activities under such programs prioritized?
  For example, if the program was applicable in more than
  one work center, how was the first work center to benefit
  from this program?

Synchronous Manufacturing is a management philosophy which
provides the umbrella under which all the other programs, such as
Automation and Quality, will be implemented. It provides answers
to the following questions:

- Which programs are appropriate for achieving the competitive
  goals?
- What areas of the plant offer the greatest opportunity?
- Where should they be implemented first?
- What is the impact of the proposed change on the plant as a
  whole?

The analysis in the preceding chapters has pointed out that the
traditional cost-based system does not provide us with very reliable
answers to these questions. Is it surprising then, that many productivity
programs have not lived up to their expectations? Is it surprising that
after the programs have been implemented at considerable effort and
expense, the results somehow fall short? Is it surprising that many of
the programs that we intuitively feel must be implemented for us to
remain competitive, such as "Quality Is Job One", have to be
implemented outside the framework of traditional methods of analysis?

And even these programs do not result in benefits as quickly as we would expect, because the focus of the implementation is often incorrect. We must appeal to the global approach inherent in Synchronous Manufacturing to adequately answer these questions.

Synchronous Manufacturing is not a program. It is the background philosophy under which conventional programs are analyzed and implemented. Without the kind of focus and impetus Synchronous Manufacturing is able to provide, most programs will not meet expectations of success or potentiality.

The phenomenal success at Bearington was achieved through the development and implementation of a manufacturing strategy along the lines outlined in Chapter Ten. What are the organizational issues involved in implementing such a basic change? What are some effective ways to address such issues?

12
Competitiveness Regained

Acknowledging The Problem

The process of regaining competitiveness begins with one vital realization: The fundamental assumptions in the current approach to managing a Manufacturing business must be critically analyzed. The Bearington plant was shocked into re-examining the very foundations of its decision-making systems and procedures because of the threat that it would be shut down in three months. Whatever his belief about the eventual success of the programs he was undertaking at Bearington to improve productivity, Alex Rogo realized that they certainly would not help him achieve such a quick turn around. Surely, but slowly, the same need to take a fresh look is being recognized by more and more people both in industry and academia. This realization stems from the fact that many of the attempts to improve productivity have not been as successful as expected and have raised serious questions about whether more of the same medicine will result in more of the same slow cure.

The search for a way to save their plant and their livelihoods led Bearington management to an understanding of Synchronous Manufacturing. The new set of operational measurements, T, I and OE, exposed the fact that current management practices and decision-making techniques were not serving them well. Jonah helped them realize that the basic phenomena of manufacturing, Statistical Fluctuations and Dependent Events (or interactions), render the assumptions of the traditional cost system invalid. Their previous understanding of productivity was erroneous and in many instances the decisions they had made in order to improve productivity had actually contributed to a deterioration of the plant's performance.

A Solution   The solution came from an understanding of the impact of Statistical Fluctuations and Dependent Events in a manufacturing operation. The fundamental realization was that not all elements within the plant are of equal value in their impact on the whole operation. Some elements were constraints and others were non constraints. They had to recognize which elements were which and manage them accordingly. Using systematic procedures, the Bearington plant management recognized the constraints to their ability to ship on time - to improve Throughput - were two capacity constraints or Bottlenecks.

Detailed procedures for the management of theconstraints and non-constraints were then established. The procedures were derived from an analysis of the overall business objectives and the nature of the resource-product interactions in their manufacturing operation. In the Bearington plant this resulted in the detailed steps discussed in Chapters Eight and Nine. Using the systematic procedures that have been developed for the different categories of plants (V, A and T) the same can be quickly and methodically done for any manufacturing business. Since the the direct focus of this effort is the major business objective and the full impact of the complexity of the manufacturing operation has been recognized, the results are immediate and quite significant.

A Major Obstacle   The only major obstacle to achieving the results in the Bearington plant was the traditional system used to evaluate manufacturing managers at all levels. The traditional system sought to achieve local optimums as defined by their contribution to the cost of their operation, while Synchronous Manufacturing seeks to achieve a global

tion, while Synchronous Manufacturing seeks to achieve a global optimum for the entire operation. The two systems did not always evaluate actions the same way. Many actions that contributed to an improved performance as measured by T, I and OE resulted in an increase in the local cost of that operation. What looked good from a Synchronous Manufacturing standpoint did not always look good from a local cost standpoint.

Action Item 12.1

> Consider one of the actions undertaken at the Bearington plant (reducing the Batch sizes, letting workers stand idle at the Heat Treat waiting for the cycle to complete, etc.).
> * How would your cost system evaluate such an action?

This is a serious obstacle to the successful adoption of Synchronous Manufacturing techniques in most manufacturing operations. Alex Rogo's approach was to conceal the details of his actions from divisional and corporate management. This, of course included their impact on the accounting numbers used to measure performance at various supervisory levels. In most manufacturing companies, such an approach would lead to far more serious consequences for the plant management than Alex Rogo experienced. This is one aspect of implementing Synchronous Manufacturing techniques that must be handled differently.

Action Item 12.2

> * What would the reaction of your corporate/division be if the operating units tried the same 'trick' as Alex Rogo?

In fact, even at Bearington, all of the gains were almost lost in the end when these actions were accidentally discovered by Mr. Hilton Smyth, the Director of Productivity. At the end of the story, Alex was trying to explain the rationale for his actions to Hilton Smyth beginning with the fact that the traditional system was based on invalid assumptions. Of course he found the job difficult. He was trying to defend his actions after being "caught red-handed". Based on our experience with senior operations and financial executives, the situation would have been entirely different if Alex had undertaken his program for saving the Bearington plant with the concurrence and support of the senior managers. The tension between the Plant and the Division, reflecting a situation that is not uncommon, added interest to the story. For successful implementation in reality, this problem is better addressed at the beginning of the program, rather than at the end.

The analysis of Synchronous Manufacturing implementation at Bearington shows that in general, successful implementation requires three major elements:

1. <u>Proper Environment:</u> This is the responsibility of the senior executives. It begins with the acknowledgement that fundamental changes in management's approach to the manufacturing operation are necessary. The control systems used to set goals, to measure performance and to reward people are based on the traditional local cost concept. To implement Synchronous Manufacturing this must be replaced with a system that is based on T, I and OE. The financial systems in place today serve two needs. One is to meet regulatory requirements for reporting details about the operation to different agencies. The second is to serve as a tool to assist in internal managerial decision-making. It is the second ele-

ment that Synchronous Manufacturing concepts challenge. Financial decision-making must be done using a system based on T, I and OE: not one that is based on cost.

To create the proper environment the senior executives must:

a. Understand the concepts and their implications at a strategic level. The responsibility for establishing the manufacturing and sales strategies clearly rests with them. As we have seen, Synchronous Manufacturing provides us with a different approach to the development of the overall business strategy. Senior executives must not only understand why and how these strategies are developed, but also the difference with traditional methods for developing business strategies.

b. Understand where and why current company policies are in conflict with the overall business objectives. These policies and procedures will clearly have to be modified. The responsibility for working out the details lies with the operating units and the staff members. The senior executives must have sufficient understanding of Synchronous Manufacturing concepts to review the new policies and to provide guidelines to the operating managers. They must understand the shortcomings of the present system and be able to establish proper goals and measures for the different functions within the business. This may be as simple as changing the emphasis on the several measures currently used to evaluate a unit or a manager. It may mean realigning responsibilities for the different elements of the business, such as assigning finished goods inventories to Sales and Marketing.

c. Communicate the business goals to the organization and why this approach was chosen. Synchronous Manufacturing requires that each employee think differently about a good portion of their daily activities. Such a basic and pervasive change is greatly facilitated by frequent and visible support from the senior executives.

Leadership

2. The second major element required for successful implementation of Synchronous Manufacturing is <u>Leadership or Driving Force.</u> At Bearington, Alex Rogo clearly provided this driving force. In most organizations this will be the responsibility of the operating managers in charge of a Strategic Business Unit or the equivalent. They must provide the momentum for the program. Synchronous Manufacturing requires that a multitude of different tasks be undertaken. It is their responsibility to focus the efforts of the organization so as to maximize the results.

To provide the required Leadership and Driving Force, the operating unit managers must:

a. Understand the concepts and techniques in considerable detail. They have the responsibility to plan, execute and control the implementation program. It is also their responsibility to sustain the momentum for continually seeking to improve the performance of their units. As seen in the preceding eleven chapters, successful implementation requires the execution of many different tasks. The overall business objectives must be translated into operational terms specific to that operation. Constraints to reaching these goals must be identified. The details of the resource-product interactions in the plant and the location of the constraints must be matched with the business goals to establish the required improvements. The proper operating rules for the constraints as well as the non-constraints must be understood. The critical control points must be determined so that the execution of the plan can be controlled with minimum effort. This is crucial to success since it is a virtual impossibility to monitor the myriad of details.

b. Develop internal performance measurements. The major responsibility of the operating managers is to change the focus of the employees from their own local areas to the needs of the entire operation. This cannot be done if current performance measures, which are local in view, remain in place. Performance measurements that reflect the needs of the entire operation must be developed and implemented. In most cases, it is our experience that this is more a change in emphasis or the priority of different measures, than it is a completely new set of measures. Most financial systems are designed to collect the information needed to support Synchronous Manufacturing. The measures that support Synchronous Manufacturing receive a lower priority today in relation to those that affect cost, such as labor variance and utilization. The operation managers, along with the division or corporate management must resolve any conflicts that may arise between these internal measurements and company policies. A good example of such a conflict is the result of the batch size reductions undertaken at Bearington. It was Alex Rogo's responsibility to resolve with Bill Peach, Hilton Smyth and Ethan Frost, the need to reduce batch sizes in order to improve delivery times and the effect this would have on the unit cost of the product.

Knowledge
Of The How To

3. The third element required for successful implementation of Synchronous Manufacturing is to transfer the <u>Knowledge of the Concepts and Techniques</u> to all of the line and staff managers of the operating unit and to make sure that this knowledge is transformed into their behavior patterns. In the Bearington plant, the knowledge had to be transferred to all of the managerial personnel from shop operations, production and inventory control, maintenance, engineering, finance and systems. As we saw in Chapter Seven, the transition from knowledge to action and behavior, requires that the method of transfer meet four basic requirements.

    a.   The knowledge must be transferred using formal theory and examples from the environment. This was done by Jonah during his two visits to Bearington and the several telephone conversations with Alex Rogo.

    b.   The knowledge should be immediately applied in their day-to-day activities. It is only when we try to apply these concepts that the difficult questions surface. For example, the Bearington managers "understood" the concept of Bottlenecks, but when they were faced with identifying and managing the Bottlenecks, cogent questions were raised.

    c.   The questions raised above must be resolved quickly. Otherwise, the doubts raised in the initial attempts at application will solidify and with no alternate course of action, managers will return to their old mode of behavior. This is why Jonah himself made a trip to Bearington, as soon as the managers faced the problem of managing the Bottlenecks. Jonah did the same thing when the total focus on the Bottleneck and its parts created a confusing situation.

d. There must be motivation to make this behavior modification. This is done through the actions of the operating managers and the senior executives of the company. The new performance measures and the visible support of these senior managers, as well as a clear understanding of the problem and the new solution, are the necessary elements in creating a strong motivation. Of course, as the implementation progresses, the positive feedback created by the successful results and maintained by peer pressure will sustain the process. Here again it is the responsibility of the plant and senior management to exploit this positive atmosphere to attain increasingly higher levels of performance. We see this clearly at Bearington where toward the end, each employee was actively searching for ways to improve the company. This is in strong contrast to the situation we find most often where the factory worker is motivated to do the least possible. Nothing breeds successful employee involvement more than the success of the business through the actions of the employees.

When Synchronous Manufacturing technology is successfully transferred to an organization (as Alex Rogo was able to accomplish at Bearington with Jonah's help) the impact on the organization is profound. The true measure of Bearington's resurrection was not in the immediate impact on the bottom line. It is true that this was the measure that the corporation used in their decision to keep the Bearington plant operational and the impact on the bottom line was significant indeed. The true measure of Bearington's resurrection, however, is the renewed vitality of the plant. The plant had been united by more than just the effort to stay alive. The processes by which they understood how they had lost their competitive position and by which they were able to achieve the rapid improvements required for survival are based on the explicit recognition that manufacturing is an interdependent and dynamic world. Synchronous Manufacturing recognizes that a plant with very successful local empires is doomed to fail. The entire philosophy is based on recognizing and understanding the common goal. Due to this focus on a common goal, conflicts are minimized and can be resolved rationally. Naturally, unity of the organization is achieved. By aggressively searching out the constraints to improving the overall business performance, Synchronous Manufacturing continually leverages the entire operation. The result is a rapid and continual improvement, as we have seen in the case of Bearington. This lifts the spirits of those in the organization, resulting in greater unity and a renewed commitment to achieve even higher levels of performance. So, we find that competitiveness can not only be regained, it can be also be sustained.

Appendix A -1
Narrative Summary
Chapters 1,2,3

1

Alex Rogo, Plant Manager, arrives at the Bearington plant of UniWare Division of UniCo at his usual early hour, to find the Mercedes of the Division Vice-President, Bill Peach, parked in Alex's reserved space. This upsets him. He believes that this is another crude demonstration of power by his superior. Reading the "NUMBER 1" on the license plate of Bill Peach's car, Alex thinks that his boss will do anything to anyone to become the CEO of UniCo. He parks in the Controller's reserved spot. Then, as Alex approaches the plant, four excited men, the shift supervisor, a department foreman, the union steward and a machine operator, burst out, shouting angrily at one another. Alex approaches them and attempts to calm the men somewhat. He learns from them that Bill Peach had arrived about an hour earlier. Acting extremely abrasively toward all whom he encountered, Bill had hurried around the plant expediting a hot order. Because of Bill's behavior, the union steward is threatening a walkout. Alex cools the situation for the moment and enters the plant to find Bill Peach.

Bill Peach is waiting in Alex's office. He tells Alex that the order he is expediting is for one of UniCo's biggest customers, Bucky Burnside. Burnside is livid at consistently poor deliveries from the Bearington plant in general, and Order 41427 in particular. The order is so critical that Bill Peach had to take the responsibility for expediting it himself, since he was unsuccessful in reaching Alex at home the previous evening. Alex did not tell Bill that he had not answered the phone because he and his wife were arguing. Alex apologizes and promises to expedite the order personally. But, he tells Peach, to improve performance in general, he must replace the workers lost in a second forced lay-off three months earlier. Bill strongly disagrees with Alex and his analysis. He accuses him of running an inefficient plant. He says that he once thought that Alex Rogo was *the* manager with the capability to turn the floundering Bearington operation around. But Alex is failing, and the Bearington plant has the worst performance in the entire UniWare division. He tells Alex that he has only three months to turn a profit or the plant will be closed. When Bill Peach finally leaves, Alex goes into the plant (an environment he obviously enjoys) to investigate for himself the problems with Burnside's order. He meets Bob Donovan, the veteran Production Manager.

Alex is first stunned, then angered to learn from Bob that the NCX-10, the complex machine necessary to produce a needed part, has been damaged through operator error and is down for repair.

2

Alex Rogo drives home early that evening to eat a quick dinner before returning to the plant. It is only when he sees that Julie has arranged for a baby sitter and is dressed for an evening out that he realizes that he has forgotten the promise of a night out he made after the argument of the previous evening. He asks Julie for a postponement, telling her that he must return to work. Julie becomes upset at being "stood up" again. Alex tries to excuse himself by telling Julie that Bill Peach has threatened to close the plant. Julie tells Alex that she is unhappy in Bearington because she has not fit in socially and because he has been neglecting her. She begins to cry. Alex promises to take her out the following night. He hurries back to the plant, his appetite gone.

During the drive, Alex reflects on his strong feelings for the town of Bearington, the town in which he was born and raised. It pains him to think of how much the town's industrial base has eroded since the mid-1970's. To him it seems that plants have been closing down and moving out at the rate of one per year. And now he is concerned that his plant will be next.

At the plant, Bob Donovan informs him that it is still "touch and go" to ship Order 41427. Alex feels that he is living a manager's nightmare as he watches what seems like the entire work force focus on shipping just one order. He agonizes over a complete breakdown of efficiency as production workers hand carry parts and assemblies "one at a time" through each operation. When the order finally ships just past 11:00 P.M., Alex invites Bob out for something to eat. Over hamburgers and beer, and using the Burnside order as a starting point, Alex and Bob discuss the constant conflict between two very real demands: the demand to flow material quickly through the plant and the demand to run a low cost, efficient operation.

Afterwards, Alex returns to the plant, sits in his office and wonders what it is that is so wrong in the Bearington plant. By all measurements of cost reduction and efficiencies, his should be a profitable operation. Yet, Bearington is drowning in red ink and is in danger of going under completely. And he does not know what to do to prevent it. It is very late when a very tired Alex Rogo leaves for home and a short rest.

3

The sun is just rising as Alex drives to work the next morning. He becomes angry at the all-consuming demands of the plant that allow him no time to relax and enjoy the world that is now awakening around him. He recalls the friendship that, until recently, existed between him and Bill Peach.

On the way to a divisional performance meeting, Alex meets Nathan Selwin, a friend who is on Peach's staff. Nathan confides that the entire Division is to be sold if Peach cannot improve performance by the year's end. Alex realizes that he "could be out on the street" should Bearington fold. In the meeting, Bill Peach and Ethan Frost, the Division Controller, present the frightful vision of the business running out of cash. They urge cutting expenses and improving productivity, but Alex has been shaken and is not really listening. Struggling to pay attention, he reaches into his jacket pocket for a pen. Instead he finds a cigar, and for a moment he can't remember where it came from. Then he begins to remember.

Appendix A -2
Narrative Summary
Chapters 4,5

4

The cigar triggers memories of a chance meeting at O'Hare Airport with one of his former professors, Jonah. Alex had struck up a conversation with Jonah but, until he mentioned that he was a Plant Manager for UniCo, Jonah seemed bored. Then Alex mentioned that he was travelling to speak at a symposium on Robotics because his plant had the most experience with robots of all the UniCo facilities. Jonah asked if the robots had increased productivity in Alex's plant. When Alex said "yes", Jonah proceeded with a line of questioning that both troubled and intrigued Alex. *Did the plant make more money? Did the plant ship more product? Did the plant reduce the workforce? Did inventories go down?* Alex answered in the negative, and Jonah challenged him on his assertion that his plant was more productive because of robotics. Jonah challenged Alex's concept of productivity.

Alex finally responded by telling Jonah that his efficiencies were up and his costs were down - two key competitive measurements. But Jonah was not impressed. He kept Alex on the defensive by suggesting to him that his inventories had risen and that he was having trouble making scheduled shipping dates. Alex admitted that this is true, and wonders how Jonah came to know so much about the

Bearington operation. Jonah informed him that his area of study was no longer physics but a new branch of science, *the science of manufacturing organizations*. He told Alex that if he would only *think* of the things that they had been discussing then he would be able to work his plant out of trouble.

Quickly Alex replied that he never said that his plant was in trouble. Jonah contradicted him, saying that the very things that he had told him indicated serious problems in the Bearington plant. Jonah accused him of accepting things without question and thereby running a very *inefficient* operation guided by an invalid measurement *system*.

Alex and Jonah argue about the definition of productivity. Jonah made him admit that *productivity is accomplishing something in terms of a goal*. Alex seized this idea to advance his original arguments, for managing for efficiencies, as being productive since they meet company goals. Jonah interrupted him and stated that *his basic problem was that he did not know the definitive goal of any manufacturing organization*. Alex offered several company "goals": producing efficiently, power, market share. Jonah accepted none of them.

Jonah boarded his flight without telling Alex what the goal of his company should be. Although he has asked for the answer, Jonah told him to find the answer himself.

5

Alex Rogo's memory of his meeting with Jonah fades and he finds himself back in the middle of Bill Peach's divisional meeting. He listens to the flow of discussion and is struck by the feeling that what is being said is no longer relevant to him. He is convinced that no one attending, himself included, really understands what is happening at Bearington. As he listens to the business discussion around him, Alex starts to believe that Jonah may have been closer to the truth than he had originally thought. He is troubled by the fact that no one has even asked a question as basic as, "What is the Goal?". Alex senses that attending this meeting is a waste of time. Will the meeting do anything, he wonders, to make him more effective as a manager—or even save his job? During a coffee break, Alex Rogo picks up his briefcase and leaves.

But, he does not return to the Bearington plant. Instead, he drives for a while then buys a pizza and some beer. He takes the food and drink to a hill overlooking his plant. He feels he must determine the answer to the question that Jonah left with him. What is the goal of a manufacturing organization? Alex considers many possibilities: economical purchasing, supplying jobs, producing a product, quality and efficiency, technology, sales. But, although he admits that all are necessary for a successful business, he dismisses each of them in turn as the basic goal. Suddenly, Alex understands that *the real goal is to make money!* All the other things he had considered were just *means to achieve* that goal.

And what of productivity? If the goal is to make money, then any "action that moves us toward making money is productive." And the converse is true; any action not assisting in making money is not productive.

Appendix A -3
Narrative Summary
Chapters 6,7,8

6

Alex Rogo returns to the plant late in the afternoon. In order to "take a fresh look at things," he begins a walk through the plant. He encounters three second shift workers sitting idle, reading newspapers. Alex finds their supervisor and angrily demands to know why some of his workers are doing nothing. The supervisor tells him that the schedules are nearly current and that the workers are waiting for more parts. Alex reprimands the supervisor, telling him that if he cannot keep his workers busy then he will lose them to a department that can. However, as he walks away, Alex begins to have second thoughts about the instructions he just gave.

Alex wonders if those three workers, who are no longer idle, are now doing anything to make Bearington money. Did his orders to work on something make them productive according to his new understanding of the word? He observes that, as usual, most of the workers in the plant *are* working. Why isn't the plant making money? He is also struck with the staggering complexity of his manufacturing operation, of any manufacturing organization. He despairs at the prospect of controlling the myriad of production activities in the shop. It has suddenly become very difficult, if not impossible, for Alex to perceive any connection between his current performance measurements, like product cost and direct labor variances, and the decisions necessary to improve productivity in the plant.

Returning to his office, Alex finds his desk littered with call back messages from Bill Peach. Reluctantly he dials Peach's number. He is relieved when there is no answer. Hanging up, he turns his thoughts once again to the problem of valid, simplified methods of determining productivity when Lou, the Plant Controller, enters.

After some conversation about Bill Peach and information updates that he needs, Alex asks Lou if he agrees that the goal of the Bearington plant is to make money. Alex briefly recounts to Lou the line of reasoning that prompted him to ask the question. Then he asks how he can know if he is making money. They discuss *net profit* (NP) as one measure. But Lou tells Alex that net profit is not enough, since it is an absolute measurement. A relative measurement is also needed, and they conclude that *return on investment* (ROI) is appropriate. But these two are still not enough, Lou insists. Without cash, even a company that shows a profit and has a good ROI cannot exist. Rogo and Lou agree that *cash flow* (CF), a measure of survival, should be the third and final financial measurement. During their conversation Lou senses Alex's worry, and asks if Bearington is dropping dangerously below the cash flow survival line.

Alex relates the conversation with Bill Peach and the threat of closing the plant in three months. Lou argues with him that the problem is not with the measurements. Union problems, employee apathy, and deteriorating quality are the real reasons for Bearington's failure, Lou contends. Alex wonders as he listens. If Lou and so many smart people like him seem to know all the answers, why is the plant and the division failing more each day?

After Lou leaves, Alex writes Net Profit, Cash Flow and Return On Investment on a pad and considers what he has discovered. It occurs to him that the plant would really be making money if he could have all three measurements *increase simultaneously*. Alex writes this as his restated goal.   He realizes that continued reliance on conventional measurements would only continue producing conventional results. And those results have been disastrous. He wants some new communication between the shop floor decision making and his three financial measurements of making money. Unable to think of any measurements that would suffice, he begins to research his textbooks. He searches until late that night but finds nothing useful.

Julie is angry when Alex calls her. He had forgotten about the postponed evening out. He can say nothing to improve the situation. He tells Julie that he will be home in an hour. Sarcastically, she tells him not to rush. Alex resigns himself to domestic misery.

Alex takes one last walk into the plant before leaving. He meets the second shift supervisor, Eddie. Eddie irritates him because he never deviates from what is proper and expected. Alex dubs him Mr. Regularity. On a whim, Alex asks Eddie what he is doing for the company in terms of Net Profit, Return On Investment and Cash Flow. Eddie is unable to respond except in terms of the traditional measurements with which he is accustomed. He speaks of labor hours and parts per shift. Alex cannot find a way to relate the detail of the shop floor to the global goal of making money.

7

Alex Rogo returns home late. His family is asleep, but Julie, although angry, has left him dinner. His daughter, Sharon, comes into the kitchen to show him her straight A report card. Sharon grows tired as they talk and Alex carries her back to bed. He is alone again.

Alex is troubled and wrestles with his course of action. Should he persist at the Bearington plant or should he begin searching for another job, in another town? No. Alex vows to do the best he can in the next three months at the plant. But, he wonders what he can do by himself. As he lies in bed unable to sleep, he decides that he must again talk to Jonah.

8

At the plant the following day, Alex Rogo is first reprimanded by Peach for his early departure from the meeting the day before, then engaged in a series of meetings that last until the evening. As he is driving home, he remembers his plan to try to find Jonah. He detours to his mother's house. Alex spends hours searching for his old address book. It is 1:00 A.M. when he finally finds it. Oblivious to the lateness of the hour, he makes a call to a friend from his university days who knows where Jonah might be reached. After more hours of calls, messages and waiting, Jonah contacts Alex. The two men pick up the conversation begun at the airport.

When Jonah asks, Alex tells him that he thinks that the goal of a manufacturing organization is to make money. He is pleased when Jonah agrees with him. Alex tells Jonah that he has come to distrust the value of his current measurements system as a tool to guide him in being productive, in moving toward the goal. Again, Jonah agrees. He tells Alex that he will give him three measurements that will allow him to develop operational rules for managing the Bearington plant.

Jonah gives Alex very precise definitions of Throughput, Inventory and Operating Expense. Jonah is in a hurry, but he takes the time to give Alex some further advice. Jonah tells Alex to be concerned with results for the entire organization. He must consider the global impact of his actions and not dwell on local optimums.

Alex Rogo still does not know how to develop operational rules, even with the new definitions. But, Jonah is pressed for time. He asks for a number where Alex may be reached. An exhausted Alex Rogo falls asleep in his old bedroom for the balance of the morning.

Appendix A -4
Narrative Summary
Chapters 9,10

9

Still at his mother's house, Alex Rogo wakes up late in the morning and calls into the plant. Fran, his secretary, relays some plant news to him and then tells him that J. Bart Granby, the Chairman of the Board of UniCo, is coming to the plant sometime soon to film a piece on productivity and robotics. Alex is aghast. When his mother asks him what is wrong, he briefly explains and tells his mother that the robots don't "work" in the plant the way they were intended. His mother gives him some advice on his hectic life style and Alex leaves for his home. Julie is not there when he arrives.

While at home, Alex realizes that the three measurements of Throughput, Inventory and Operating Expense are related to the three questions that Jonah had asked at the airport during their conversation. Has Bearington sold any more product? Has inventory gone down? Did Bearington lay off any workers? Alex understands that throughput should go up and inventory and operating expense should go down. These three things should occur simultaneously, just as Net Profit, Return On Investment and Cash Flow should go up simultaneously. Alex decides to test his ideas by analyzing the impact of the robots in the plant, but he is stumped as to how to go about it.

Alex arrives at the plant early in the afternoon. He asks Lou to interrupt what he is doing for Bill Peach and work with him for awhile. Together they check to see if sales have increased since the robots went on line. Lou checks his information and finds that sales have not increased, but have remained stable. They do discover, however, that past due shipments have increased. Next, Alex asks about inventory of those parts that are processed by the robots.

Lou is unable to answer, so they call in Stacey Potazenik, the Inventory Control Manager. After explaining to Stacey what they need, she tells Alex and Lou that she is sure that the inventory of those parts processed on the robots has gone up. She tells them that the efficiencies on the robots had been too low, so she had been forced to release more material for machining. The surplus of parts could not be consumed because there were no orders or there were shortages of other parts at assembly. In order to find why there are parts shortages, Bob Donovan, the Production Manager, is called in. It is not necessarily the lack of parts that is the problem, Bob says, *it is the lack of the right parts at the right time.*

10

Alex Rogo begins to explain that running to efficiencies may keep the calculated costs down, but can hurt the company in a stable or depressed market. But, his staff is confused, so he offers to recount what he has learned.

After Alex explains, there is a flurry of questions about the three new measurements. He responds that the three measurements, just like the goal, are related to money - money coming into the system, money being used within the system, and money paid out of the system. Lou suggests that employee time is Operating Expense, which simplifies the accounting. It reduces the need for number games. Lou also states that *it is the market that determines the value of product, not the accounting system.*

Bob is not convinced, and begins to list items that he believes are not covered by the three new measurements. He mentions tools, machines, the physical plant, scrap and even the Chairman's chauffeur. But, as the staff examines each item, they find that they do in fact fall logically and readily into the measurement system that Alex has just explained. Then Alex states that the way the Bearington plant has been using the robots is not only non-productive, it is *counter-productive* to increasing profits.

Alex discusses the ultimatum that Peach has given him. He admits that he doesn't know if they can turn the plant around, but at least now he knows what they have been doing wrong. Alex and his staff agree that Jonah should be contacted again. Jonah is located at a hotel in New York. Arrangements are made for Alex to meet with him there in the morning.

Appendix A -5
Narrative Summary
Chapters 11-17

11

Alex Rogo, having made arrangements to meet Jonah at his hotel in New York the next morning, returns home to pack. He and Julie renew their running domestic battle. Julie tells Alex that he is too absorbed in his job. She complains that his continuous neglectful behavior has unfairly disrupted their family life.

But Alex has neither the time nor the inclination to argue the point. He finishes packing and leaves for the airport. When Alex arrives at his hotel that evening he calls his home repeatedly, but the phone rings unanswered. He has no idea where Julie has gone.

Alex meets Jonah early the next morning. Jonah asks him why he has taken the trouble to track him down and meet with him. Alex tells him of the three month deadline at the Bearington facility and asks for his help in saving the plant. Jonah explains that he is much too busy and couldn't possibly dedicate his time to help Alex. But, he goes on to say, he thinks that Alex could help himself, with some guidance. Alex understands that he has nothing to lose, so he agrees to follow Jonah's proposal.

Alex and Jonah proceed to review what Alex has learned. Jonah expands and clarifies some of the issues: Efficiencies and productivity, excess inventory as an effect or symptom, the need to improve

Throughput while reducing Inventory and Operating Expense *simultaneously* . Jonah also discusses some new ideas of manufacturing relationships. He tells Alex that the more a company tries to *balance capacity* in a plant, the closer that company will be to bankruptcy. Alex does not understand. Jonah states that the basic assumption of almost all Western manufacturing is that Throughput will not go down and Inventory will not go up if capacity is trimmed to market demand. Jonah states that this is completely wrong. Jonah says that it can be mathematically proven that if capacity is reduced to equal marketing demand then Throughput must go down and Inventory must go up. And, if Inventory goes up, then Operating Expense must increase as well. This is why, Jonah observes, no company has ever succeeded in running a "balanced plant". Jonah discourses on the phenomena of *Statistical Fluctuation* and *Dependent Events*. He defines Statistical Fluctuations as those types of information which vary from one instance to the next. Jonah defines Dependent Events as those which cannot take place unless a prior event is completed.

Alex still questions Jonah. He tells Jonah that he accepts the existence of these two phenomena, but he does not understand how either can adversely affect his plant. Jonah tells him that statistical fluctuations and dependent events must be considered *together,* and not separately. Alex still does not understand and becomes very upset when Jonah abruptly leaves, instructing Alex to contact him again after he understands the impact of the combination of these two phenomena.

12

As Alex drives home from the airport, he is troubled by thoughts of his wife leaving him. But, he finds Julie in the kitchen. He asks her where she had been the night before. She tells Alex that she had spent the night with her friend, Jane, whom she had known prior to the move to Bearington. Alex is amazed that she had driven so far. Julie tells her husband that she needed someone to talk to. Alex and Julie discuss the situation at the plant. He asks her to put up with his behavior and long hours for the next two months. They look forward to having a good weekend together.

13

All of Alex's plans for a nice, quiet weekend with the whole family go by the boards early Saturday morning. Davey, his son, wakes Alex to remind him of the promise to go along on an overnight Boy Scout hike. To his dismay, Alex discovers that he is the only adult marching with the troop.

The march is to cover ten miles through woodland trails, ending at a prearranged campsite. Alex assigns one scout, Ron, to lead, telling him to set an easy pace. He then instructs all the other boys to stay in single file and not pass anyone. He figures that the march should take no longer than five hours, since the column seems to be moving at a comfortable pace of about two miles per hour. As he walks, Alex is preoccupied with several concerns. First, he thinks of Julie and how this hike had devastated their plans. Then, Alex thinks about the discussion he had in New York with Jonah. He puzzles over Dependent Events and Statistical Fluctuations, and what Jonah was trying to have him understand.

Dependent Events, he knows, is no more than the fact that step one of a process must be finished before step two can begin. In fact, he thinks, this dependency is apparent in many things besides manufacturing. It could be applied to the very hike that he is supervising. In order for a hiker to walk the trail, the boys in front have to walk it first. But what of Statistical Fluctuations? Over the course of the hike, Alex expects that while each individual stride may vary and that the scout may, at times, be travelling at 1.5 miles per hour or 2.5 miles per hour, he should *average* 2 miles per hour for *the entire march*. And he thinks that the same should apply in the plant. He believes that, although the length of each operation on each part cannot be predicted in advance, the average length of a manufacturing run could be accurately predicted. He can find nothing wrong with his logic. While climbing a hill, Alex realizes that the column has slowed down behind a boy named Herbie. Soon the crest of the hill is reached and Alex observes that the troop is now spread out over a half mile. Herbie, and the group behind him, begin to run, but it is soon apparent that they will not be able to catch up. Alex orders the column to halt.

Alex asks Ron why he didn't set a moderate pace. Ron replies that he did. After a short rest the march starts again. But this time Alex is watching the progress very closely. Soon the column begins to spread, just as it did before. Then Alex realizes the problem inherent with Dependent Events in conjunction with Statistical Fluctuations. Any hiker can always go slower, but with the exception of Ron at the head of the line, each hiker can go no faster than the person in front of him. Therefore, it is easier to lose ground than to make it up. The fluctuations do not average out, they accumulate.

In his mind, he takes what he has discovered and applies it to the plant environment. He makes an analogy of the marching troop. Each marcher is a resource consuming material, the ground that is being covered. Ron, the first "resource", puts inventory into the system as he walks the trail. The trail is "sold" as it is walked by the last marcher and becomes Throughput. As Alex considers the validity of his analogy, the troop halts for lunch.

14

Although it is noon and time for lunch, Alex realizes that he and the scouts have not travelled nearly far enough. Sandwiches are eaten while Alex wrestles with the problem of the balanced system. Is his analogy of the scout troop really valid? He notices one of the boys with some dice and the idea of a game develops. Alex uses match sticks for inventory and the dice for resources. He gathers five of the boys to play the game. Each of them represents a resource processing match sticks, and the match sticks must pass through each operation in turn. The game progresses with unexpected results. Throughput is down while Inventory in the system has increased dramatically. If the principles affecting the dice game are really at work in the plant, he concludes, that the *difference* between *what is expected* and *what will actually happen* on the shop floor could spell disaster for the company. He suspects that the similarities between the model and the gloomy situation at the Bearington plant are too close to be coincidental. His curiosity peaked, Alex decides to investigate further.

15

Lunch has ended, and Alex and the troop are once again on the march. He is still bothered by what he has seen and learned. Alex has identified the cause of the troop's problem. Some of the boys do not have the extra capacity or speed necessary to catch up when they fall behind. Alex is reminded of a mathematical principle learned in college that deals with linear dependencies involving two or more variables. And Alex begins to see similarities between running to catch up on the hike and "running" to catch up at the plant.

Alex notices that he and Herbie are at the end of the column, and that the troop is strung out worse than ever. In addition, only five miles (half the march) have been covered in five hours. At this rate, Alex figures, the campsite would not be reached until dark. He halts the line and tells all the boys to join hands. Then he takes Herbie and walks him to the front of the line, making him the leader while reversing the order of march. When the scouts complain Alex points out that the group is a team, and as such their goal is to arrive at their destination together. The line of marchers stays much more compact now, with no permanent gaps appearing. But the progress is still too slow.

Herbie's speed must be increased to increase the speed of the scouts. Upon examining Herbie's pack, Alex finds a whole host of items. He distributes the items among the rest of the boys. Considerably lightened, Herbie sets out at a much faster pace. The scouts cover the final four miles in two hours. Davey tells his father that he is proud of him for accomplishing something no other parent ever had. Alex had figured out how to keep everyone together while covering ground quickly. He tells his son that he learned some things that will help him run his plant.

16

Alex and his son, Davey, return home from the overnight hike. There is a note from Julie waiting for them. It announces that she has left Alex and the children. Julie wants some time to herself to consider their relationship. After picking up his daughter, Sharon, at his mother's house where Julie had left her, he tries unsuccessfully to locate his wife.   His personal life is in complete shambles.

17

The next day at the plant Alex has an urgent message to call Hilton Smyth. Hilton demands that Alex ship 100 sub-assemblies needed by his plant to ship an order and he threatens to complain to Bill Peach if he does not receive the parts by the end of the day. When the conversation ends, Alex reads a memo announcing that Hilton Smyth has been promoted to Divisional Productivity Manager.

Alex assembles his staff, which now includes Ralph Nakamura, the Manager of Data Processing, and reviews what he has learned from Jonah and the Boy Scout hike. His staff is not wholly convinced that his new approach will work. The debate is interrupted to bring Alex up to date on the progress of the parts for Smyth. It occurs to Alex that he can use the parts' expediting as an example to prove what he has been telling his staff about Dependent Events and Statistical Fluctuations. He wagers that, even though it looks like they should be finished on time, the parts will not ship on the five o' clock shuttle truck to Hilton Smyth's plant.

Each of the department heads involved is apprised of the need to produce 100 of the parts. Yet, just as Alex had predicted, the parts for shipment come up short. Only 90 pieces are finished by five o'clock.

Appendix A -6
Narrative Summary
Chapter 18

18

Alex Rogo returns home to his children and his mother, who is taking care of them while Julie is away. It is a despondent family at the meal. Davey tells him that Julie had called, but she had refused to say where she was or leave a number.

The next morning, Alex encounters a more enthusiastic staff at work. After some discussion, they decide to contact Jonah again. As the staff gathers around a speaker phone, Alex relates to Jonah what he has learned since their last conversation. Jonah offers his congratulations on the new insight they have gained.

Jonah informs them that next, resources in the plant must be identified as either Bottlenecks or Non-Bottlenecks. He tells them that capacity should not be balanced to market demand, but rather production *flow* should be balanced to customer orders. Jonah ends the phone conversation suggesting they attempt to identify the Bottlenecks in the Bearington plant. The staff sets to work.

They first attempt to calculate loads on every resource in the plant based on open sales orders and marketing forecast. But, after several days of intense and methodical effort with information supplied by Data Processing, they admit a problem. The data supplied is inaccurate. They discuss alternative approaches to the problem.

They finally conclude that there are two means of attack that could quickly provide a manageable list of potential Bottlenecks. The first would be to ask the expediters in the plant where most of the shortages and problems arise. The second approach is to look at the piles of work-in-process inventory queued up, or back logged, before each resource and to identify the largest queues. They decide to use the second approach.

Two Bottlenecks are identified: the NCX-10 machining center and the Heat Treat Furnaces. In both instances, efficiency considerations have driven management decisions that have led directly to the production problems. Alex is resigned to the fact that the sequence of operations must remain the way it is, as it would be impossible to reorganize so that the resource with the least capacity would be first in the routings. There is no hope of convincing corporate management to invest in additional resources to increase the capacity of under utilized equipment in a plant currently losing money. Alex and his staff must increase material flow through the NCX-10 and Heat Treat operations, but their success seems doubtful at this point.

Appendix A -7
Narrative Summary
Chapters 19, 20, 21

19

Julie has not returned. Alex tells Davey that he is going to pick up Jonah at the airport. He had solved the march problem by putting Herbie at the head of the line. But, in the plant the process could not be changed to put the two newly discovered Herbies at the start operations. Jonah's help was still needed. Alex has some doubts that there could be substantial improvements in his operations. *Jonah emphatically states that there are only two circumstances whereby his suggestions would not work. Firstly, there would have to be an absence of demand for the Bearington products, and secondly, his suggestions would not work if management refused to employ them.*

Jonah tells Alex and his staff that they must increase capacity of the Bottlenecks by reevaluating their management of these resources. There is available capacity on the Bottlenecks that they do not see and therefore do not use.

Jonah and the Bearington staff tour the plant, stopping first at the NCX-10. It is not in operation, and Jonah questions why. Bob Donovan explains that the machine is in the process of being setup, and that the setup men are on break. Jonah comments that they should take their break only when the machine is running. Once time is lost on a Bottleneck, it can never be recovered. A Bottleneck should *never* be idle.

At Heat Treat, Jonah looks at the large queues and asks if there is any way to offload the resource. Stacey Potazenik states that to go to a heat treat vendor would increase the unit cost of the product. Jonah questions further the concept of standard cost, then relates it to Bottleneck production. Since everything that goes through a Bottleneck can be immediately sold, the value of the items queued up is not equal to the standard cost per part, but the selling price of the product being shipped. Some quick calculations reveal that, using Jonah's logic, the total value of the parts waiting at Heat Treat is not $20,000 but $1,000,000. Alex and his staff are stunned.

Next, Jonah asks about Quality Control. Where in the process are parts inspected? He is told that they are usually inspected just before final assembly. Once again Jonah relates the discussion to management of Bottleneck resources. If an unacceptable part is not found until after processing on a Bottleneck, then that scrapped part can never be recovered. Once the time on the Bottleneck is lost, it remains lost. QC should be *before* the Bottlenecks.

The discussion of the importance of Bottlenecks continues in the office. Jonah shows Lou that the cost of a Bottleneck hour is really the cost of an hour for the entire plant. Instead of $32.50 per hour that was currently assigned, Lou is shocked to compute that the actual cost of a Bottleneck hour is $2,735. At that rate, Jonah continues, it is foolish to process parts on a Bottleneck that cannot be used for immediate Throughput.

The next morning Alex fills in his mother and his children on his progress at the plant. He tells Davey that Jonah showed them some ways to make their "Herbies" produce more. Then, Sharon tells her father that she has spoken to her mother. During the phone conversation she heard the same music that she had heard at her maternal grandparent's home. Alex kisses his daughter saying that he will give the Barnetts a call.

20

Alex Rogo calls his in-laws in an attempt to contact Julie, but Julie's mother, Ada, is not very cooperative. Accusing him of neglecting her daughter for years, she hangs up on him.

Alex convenes his ten o'clock meeting in his office. There is some agreement that what Jonah told them the day before made sense. Lou had even gone so far as to investigate and discover that only 80% of their product was affected by Bottleneck parts. This reduced the cost per Bottleneck hour to $2,188 - still an impressive figure. Ralph Nakamura and Bob Donovan remain somewhat undecided, but Stacey Potazenik argues that they have seen enough to justify the risks involved in making changes. They agree to make some operational decisions based on what Jonah has shown them.

Concentrating on the newly identified Bottlenecks they develop a management strategy that can be almost immediately implemented - move QC inspection just prior to the Bottleneck, implement new rules for lunches and breaks that will keep the Bottlenecks operating all the time, develop a priority of production across the Bottlenecks so that parts needed for the oldest orders are the first to run.

Instead of going home after work, Alex goes to the home of his in-laws in the hope that Julie is there. He goes to the door and asks for her. She does come out and they talk of their failing relationship. Julie and Alex are still in love, but she needs more from him than he has been able to give. He asks her to come home with him, fearing that continued separation will end in divorce. But Julie is still unsure and refuses. Alex tells Julie that he loves her. She kisses him and returns to her parents' house. Alex drives home.

21

Even though Alex and Julie seem to have stabilized their relationship, and may be well on the road to resolving their personal problems, he is depressed when he arrives home. He wonders what will happen if Julie asks for a divorce. He decides to take some action and calls Julie and asks her for a date. Julie quickly agrees and they make arrangements for Saturday night.

The next morning Alex and his staff meet with Ted Spencer, supervisor of Heat Treat, and Mario DeMonte, supervisor of the NCX-10. During the long previous night, Ralph Nakamura and Stacey Potazenik had worked with bills of material, inventories and past due order shortages to develop a priority list of parts for each Bottleneck area. They discovered that approximately 85% of the old orders are held for parts to be processed by one or both of the Bottlenecks.

Alex gives the two supervisors very simple explicit instructions. They are to work only on the parts that are on the lists they have been given, and only in the order in which they appear. Alex promises to protect the two men from over aggressive expediting and from demands of the sales department. He tells them that they supervise the two most important resources in the plant, and that they may very well hold the future of the Bearington facility in their hands.

After that meeting, Alex meets with Mike O'Donnell, the local union president. Mike is concerned that the company is trying to take advantage of the workers with new lunch and break rules that are very definitely against the contract. Alex briefly explains the tenuous situation at the plant. Mike tells him that he and his committee will have to consider the problem and return later with an answer.

Out in the plant, Alex finds the NCX-10 standing idle. He becomes irate and searches for Mario DeMonte, the supervisor of that department. Mario tells him that the machine is waiting for material needed to start the next job on the priority list. The NCX-10 is down because Mario is following his explicit orders. Alex modifies his instructions and tells Mario to start the next job on the list for which he has material.

Bob Donovan is somewhere in the plant trying to find the parts needed. Alex finds him in the lathe department. Bob explains that the parts needed for the NCX-10 are queued up waiting for a long lathe run to finish. No one in lathes had been informed of the importance of the parts, and the department had been following normal routine. Alex decides that they must develop a plant-wide system of communication that will identify important Bottleneck parts.

Bob Donovan is troubled that expediting Bottleneck parts will cause a drop in efficiencies at all the other resources. But Alex is adamant, and a meeting is held to explain to each employee the new priority system and the importance of the Bottlenecks. Red-tagged parts are Bottleneck parts and have priority over green-tagged parts. Also, red-tagged parts with a lower number have priority over red-tagged parts with a higher number. Before he leaves on Friday afternoon, he receives a call from Mike O'Donnell, the union president. The union will not challenge the new rules.

At 7:30 the next night Alex Rogo picks up Julie for their date.

Appendix A -8
Narrative Summary
Chapters 22, 23, 24

22

After only one week it seems to Alex Rogo and his staff that the changes they made are yielding very positive results. Twelve of the oldest orders had been shipped. The oldest order in the plant is only forty-four days past due. Only a week before the oldest was fifty-eight days past due.

The new break and lunch rules are in effect. Quality Control inspections before the Bottlenecks are identifying a significant percentage of non-conforming parts, thus saving Bottleneck time. Progress is being made, Alex admits, but it is not enough. He wants recommendations for off-loading the Bottleneck by the mid-week staff meeting.

He later meets with Elroy Langston, Quality Control Manager, and Barbara Penn, Manager of Employee Communications. Elroy explains that it is sometimes very difficult to distinguish whether or not a part has been processed through a Bottleneck. He and Barbara suggest that by marking the red tags on Bottleneck parts with yellow tape as they leave the Bottleneck, all the operators will realize that the parts must be handled and machined with special care. Alex compliments them on their initiative.

Bob Donovan calls Alex to the receiving dock. When he arrives, Bob shows him a Zmegma machine that he has borrowed from another plant. Bob explains that, using the Zmegma in combination with a couple of other resources, he can duplicate all the operations of the NCX-10.

23

As Alex Rogo is sitting in his office warmly thinking of the fun he and Julie have been having lately, manufacturing reality rears its ugly head again. A steaming Heat Treat supervisor, Ted Spencer, has come to complain that Ralph Nakamura, the Data Processing Manager has been harassing him. Alex promises to look into the situation.

When Ralph tells his story, Alex realizes that there is a serious problem. On his own initiative, Ralph has been checking differences between actual production times and estimated standard times in Heat Treat. Ted Spencer, concerned about manpower utilizations, has managed the operators at Heat Treat in such a way that material is sitting idle in this Bottleneck resource. Operators are lent to other departments during the Heat Treat cycle and no one is available to unload the equipment when the cycle is finished. Considerable time is being lost.

Alex calls in Bob Donovan. After some heated conversation, he orders Bob to have operators on duty *at all times*, even if it *seems* inefficient. Then they discuss the down time on the NCX-10. The setup personnel are very conscientious, but sometimes the resource will sit idle if setup is in process on another resource. Alex orders a machinist and a helper to be on duty at all times at the NCX-10, paralleling his instructions for Heat Treat. Bob expresses his concern about the labor reports and all this extra labor now assigned in these two areas.

At the staff meeting the next day, Bob Donovan recommends using the Zmegma and two other machines to yield 18% more of the parts processed across the NCX-10. He also recommends using an outside heat treat vendor.

His recommendations are accepted and the discussion turns to additional operator staffing. They agree to move operators from Non-Bottleneck resources to the Bottlenecks. If that movement slows the flow of material, the workers will be returned and alternates will be found.

There is a pleasant, but unexplained, production increase of ten percent during the third shift at Heat Treat that Alex decides to investigate. He comes in early one morning to talk to Mike Haley, the shift supervisor. Mike explains that he has his operators preparing loads while another is in the furnace. Alex describes this as splitting and overlapping the batches. Mike continues, showing Alex another method he is using to keep to the priority list and still take advantage of available capacity. He examines the list for items that require the same heat treat temperature as the part with the highest priority. The furnace is then loaded with as many priority items as possible on each cycle. After Mike describes an idea for reducing furnace change-over times from an hour to a few minutes, Alex moves him to the day shift and tells him that he will work on his idea with an industrial engineer.

Later, Bob Donovan informs Alex that they can change processes on some parts to eliminate the Heat Treat operation entirely. Although it will *reduce* the "efficiency" of some Non-Bottleneck operations it will paradoxically make the entire plant more productive. Alex, of course, approves the changes.

24

Things are looking up for Alex Rogo and the Bearington operation. Shipments for the month are half again greater than any month

in company history. And in the process of making all these shipments, inventory has decreased by twelve percent.

Affirmation of success comes with a phone call from Bill Peach.
He congratulates Alex for putting extra effort into improving due
date performance. Bill Peach tells him that Johnny Jons, the Marketing Manager, is very pleased as well. Alex and his staff begin a night
of celebration with champagne.

Alex has too much champagne and other samplings of good cheer.
At the end of the evening, Stacey Potazenik is the only one of the
group fit to drive since she had been drinking club soda. She offers
to drive Alex and Bob home. After dropping off Bob, Stacey continues to Alex's house. He drunkenly falls over his doorstep, tripping
Stacey as he falls. As they lie laughing on the floor, Julie, who had
been waiting to surprise him, does just that. Angry and hurt at what
she interprets as Alex's infidelity, she rushes from the house and
drives away. The next morning Julie refuses to accept his calls.

On Monday, Stacey Potazenik is waiting for him when he arrives.
She apologizes for Friday night and offers to call Julie. Alex gives
her the Barnett's telephone number. But that is not the only problem
that Stacey wants to discuss.

She tells Alex that it seems as if additional Bottlenecks have
appeared in the plant. Shortages at assembly are cropping up more
and more frequently in parts that do not cross either of the identified
Bottlenecks. Stacey is at a loss to explain the situation. Now it is the
Bottleneck parts that are waiting at assembly for Non-Bottleneck
parts. While initiating a further investigation at the plant, Alex places
a call to Jonah. During the conversation, in which he informs Jonah
what steps they have taken, Jonah offers to pay another visit to the
plant.

That night Julie calls Alex at home. Stacey Potazenik had called
her and explained the misunderstanding. Julie agrees to see him
again on Wednesday.

Appendix A -9
Narrative Summary
Chapters 25, 26

25

Jonah arrives and asks to see the Bottleneck resources. There are huge amounts of inventory queued up before the NCX-10. Jonah predicts accurately that there is a similar pile of inventory waiting at Heat Treat. Calling Bottlenecks "X" machines and Non-Bottlenecks "Y" machines, Jonah explains *the four basic relationships between the two types of resources.*

First, when a Non-Bottleneck supplies material to a Bottleneck, it must not operate at its full potential, or inventory will build up before the Bottleneck. This is because the Bottleneck, with less potential, does not have the capacity to process everything that the Non-Bottleneck can produce.

The next relationship is a Bottleneck feeding a Non-Bottleneck. The Non-Bottleneck will not be able to operate at full capacity because the Bottleneck cannot supply it sufficiently to do so.

The third relationship exists when both a Bottleneck and Non-Bottleneck provide parts to a common assembly. Since the Bottleneck production determines how many assemblies can be made, any extra production by the Non-Bottleneck will build and remain as excess inventory before final assembly.

The fourth and last of the basic relationships is that of a Bottleneck and Non-Bottleneck each supplying an independent market

demand. In the case of the Bottleneck, all production can be immediately sold and turned into Throughput. In the case of the Non-
Bottleneck, however, extra production will only remain on the shelves
as excess finished goods. Market demand limits Throughput.

Thus, the level of utilization of a Non-Bottleneck is determined
by the potential of a system constraint, *not its own potential.* Bob
Donovan, once again, objects to allowing idle time on the grounds
that efficiencies will suffer. Jonah challenges him. *Activation* of a
worker or resource just to keep efficiencies high is non-productive.
Resources must be *utilized* to bring the organization toward the goal
of making money. *Activation and utilization are not the same.*

In the drive to expedite Bottleneck parts, Non-Bottlenecks suddenly have taken the characteristics of Bottlenecks. They appear to
be Bottlenecks because Non-Bottleneck parts have been allowed to
queue up at Non-Bottleneck resources so long that there is no recov-
ery time. Thus, there is a short term, front end demand that is well in
excess of the Non-Bottleneck capacity to absorb it. It is a serious
problem, but Jonah suggests that there is a simple solution.

26

Alex Rogo discusses the solution to his problem with his children. He uses the hiking scenario again, and asks Davey and Sharon
how they would keep everyone together if Herbie were in the middle
of the column, rather than at the front. Sharon says that she would
give Herbie a drum to beat, just like in a parade. Davey says that he
would tie everyone together with ropes. Alex commends them both
and asks them what they would like for a reward for their work. They
tell him that they want their mother back.

Alex thinks back to the discussion he and his group had with
Jonah after they returned from the plant. There was agreement that

some signal from the Bottleneck to Material Release was needed. Ralph Nakamura offered a suggestion based on some work he had been doing independently. He believed that he could use data processing resources to predict, within a day or so, when material would be needed by the Bottlenecks. Based on this, Stacey Potazenik could release material. This way material release for the entire plant could be synchronized to the production capabilities of the Bottlenecks. Jonah carried this idea further and said that the same approach could also be used to determine when an order would ship, an idea that Ralph Nakamura had mentioned to Alex earlier.

Alex takes Jonah to the airport, and when he returns the next morning Bob Donovan raises another concern about efficiencies. During the inventory reduction period, idle time may increase dramatically. Stacey Potazenik comments that excess inventory ties up a lot of money. Alex authorizes the new system, even if efficiencies drop. But, he tells Bob to conceal the lower efficiency figures in the monthly report.

Appendix A -10
Narrative Summary
Chapters 27 -31

27

During a divisional managers' report meeting at corporate head-quarters, Ethan Frost and Bill Peach pay tribute to the successes of the Bearington plant. In fact, Ethan Frost states that if it were not for Bearington profits, the UniWare Division would have lost money for the seventh consecutive month. Alex Rogo has continued on his course of improvement. Bearington is completely current with customer orders. Inventory has fallen rapidly. Alex is concerned that too many standard cost accounting principles have been violated in obtaining the results at Bearington - so many, in fact, that disclosing the whole truth to Bill Peach would be inadvisable at this time.

But, there are even more urgent concerns for Alex. Bill Peach speaks privately with Alex after the meeting and tells him that he is not convinced that the progress at Bearington is permanent. He tells Alex that the only way to guarantee that the plant will not be closed is to increase profits by fifteen percent the next month. Alex realizes he must acquire more business for the plant, but he isn't sure how to go about it. He considers calling Jonah.

Later, Alex argues with Julie about the uncertain nature of their relationship. He tells her that they should start with the relationship that they have now, not with what has gone before. He goes on to say that they need some goal for their relationship and then need to decide what it is they have to do to move toward their goal.

28

Jonah calls Alex from Singapore. After Alex explains the problem, Jonah makes some suggestions. The next day Alex informs his staff of Jonah's suggestion to cut Non-Bottleneck batch sizes in half. Since inventory on Non-Bottleneck parts spend most of the time in the plant waiting for Bottleneck parts, *Bottlenecks control not only Throughput but system Inventory as well.* By cutting batch sizes in half, the amount of total time that a part spends in the plant is considerably reduced - lead time is much shorter. With a reduced lead time, the Bearington plant can capture more business, which can be translated into increased Throughput.

Alex also relates to his staff Jonah's discussion concerning the four elements of total elapsed time a given piece of material spends inside a plant. These four elements are: setup time, process time, queue time and wait time. A reduction in batch size will reduce each of these elements and hence the total manufacturing cycle time for the product.

Bob Donovan once again objects, arguing that added setups will increase the labor cost per part. Alex tells him of another thing that Jonah had told him. Since a saving on a Non-Bottleneck adds only to idle time, a saving for the system does not exist. It is a phantom saving. They agree to do the batch cutting and promise marketing a four week delivery, down from the current eight weeks.

Alex meets with Johnny Jons, the Marketing Manager. Alex tries to convince him to test the Bearington plant by promising orders for *four week* delivery. Johnny is skeptical, since he can remember in the not too distant past promising *four months* and delivering in six months, but he finally agrees.

29

Alex and Julie are spending a loving, conjugal night alone. The children are with his mother. His personal life is getting back on track, but his professional life still intrudes. When Julie asks what is bothering him he tells her it is the way he is required to apply cost measurements in the Bearington operation. The methods are in contradiction to the new and more profitable way he is running the plant. Alex is not sure what to do.

The next day Lou tells him that he may have a way around the cost problem. Even though it is against corporate policy, he offers to change the cost base to the last two months rather than the last year. That way, costs will be compared against what is currently happening in the plant.

As he finishes with Lou, Johnny Jons calls. He tells him that Bucky Burnside wants one thousand of a particular unit, and he needs delivery in two weeks. If Alex can meet the deadline Bearington may become Burnside's preferred supplier. Alex senses the urgency and promises to have an answer by the next day.

Soon, Alex and his staff have a plan of action and Alex calls Johnny Jons. They can promise to ship 250 units per week beginning in two weeks. Later, Johnny calls Alex at home to confirm receipt of the order from Burnside.

30

Several weeks later, Alex Rogo presides over another staff meeting. Not only is Burnside's order shipping on schedule, but overall plant performance has improved over the month before. Profits are higher than Bill Peach requested - they are up seventeen percent by Lou's calculations. Inventory has been reduced by sixty percent in just a few months. The new marketing strategy has brought in extra business and Throughput has doubled. Reduced batch sizes have improved flow.

When Alex is informed that Bearington is scheduled for a performance review, he looks forward to the chance to show off what has been accomplished.

Later the next week, Alex and Scott Dolin, the Personnel Manager, are out of town at a corporate meeting. When they return Bob Donovan tells Alex that while they were gone, Hilton Smyth had arrived unexpectedly to film the piece on robot productivity that Alex thought had been cancelled. Unfortunately, since inventory had been so dramatically reduced, there was no material for the celebrity robot to manipulate. Hilton Smyth suspiciously began to ask questions about batch sizing. Donovan finishes his report and Alex is uneasy.

Two days later, as an audit team visits the plant, Neil Cravitz, the assistant controller, discovers the change Lou made in the costing base. Neil Cravitz recalculates costs according to the old standards and the numbers show that costs have risen. Several days later Lou is ordered to revise the quarterly report using the old standards. The recalculation yields a profit increase of just under thirteen percent, not the seventeen percent Lou had previously computed.

Even as they are nervously pondering what this might mean, a helicopter carrying Johnny Jons and Bucky Burnside lands on the lawn outside of Alex's window. Alex briefly panics as he tries to find out if there is anything wrong with the shipments for Burnside. He learns that nothing went wrong, and when he enters the plant he finds Bucky Burnside shaking hands with each and every employee he encounters. When Burnside sees Alex he rushes to greet him. Burnside thanks Alex effusively for the performance of his plant in shipping his order. As Burnside continues through the plant, Johnny Jons tells Alex that the performance on the order has landed Bearington a long term contract, worth ten thousand units per year, from Burnside.

That evening Alex meets Julie. They go out to dinner and discuss their relationship. Julie tells Alex that she did not want their arrangement to end because she had been spending more time with him than before, and that is what she wanted all along. Alex proposes that they go to Las Vegas after his review meeting the next day and get married again. Julie appreciates the humor of the suggestion and agrees.

31

The next day Alex Rogo arrives at headquarters for the plant performance review. He is upset to find that Hilton Smyth is to conduct the meeting in place of Bill Peach. Alex argues uselessly with Smyth about the financial status of the Bearington plant. Beginning with the goal of making money, Alex tries to convince Hilton Smyth of the errors of his assumptions and the importance of Dependent Events and Statistical Fluctuations in the plant. But, after more than an hour of debate Hilton Smyth remains unconvinced. He tells Alex that no matter how he cuts it, his costs have gone up. And, he continues, if costs have increased then profits *must* have decreased. Alex is furious and as the meeting ends, he searches for Bill Peach.

Alex finds Bill Peach and follows him into his office. Alex tells him that Hilton Smyth's report on the Bearington plant will be an unfavorable one. Bill apologizes for not being at the meeting. He explains saying that he had been in conference with Board Chairman J. Bart Granby and had just been given a new corporate assignment. Alex congratulates him and asks who will be his replacement. Alex is crestfallen to learn that it will be Hilton Smyth. He voices his displeasure at being passed over. As Bill calms Alex, telling him that there is a new division being created, J. Bart Granby enters the office.

J. Bart Granby affectionately pats Alex on the back. He tells Alex that he has done more than any other manager to improve profits. He offers Alex the new divisional manager's slot, and Alex accepts.

It is a month later that Alex speaks to Jonah on the phone. Alex relates all that has happened and Jonah offers his congratulations. Alex thanks Jonah for his help, acknowledging that he would not have been able to learn everything without it. Jonah tells Alex that there is still much more to learn. Enigmatically, Jonah asks Alex to consider what his personal goals might be.

Appendix B
The Production
Dice Game*

The Production Dice Game is designed to help you understand the root causes of some of the problems in your manufacturing plants - such as too much inventory, difficulty in meeting shipment dates and the need for unplanned overtime. Most manufacturing operations share these same problems because they arise from the same causes. This dice game will help you understand these causes and also help you manage them in order to improve the performance of your plants.

All manufacturing operations share two phenomena, irrespective of the product they produce, the processes they employ and the markets they service. These are:

1. Statistical Fluctuations
2. Dependent Events

These two phenomena common to all manufacturing plants cause the performance of the plant to be less than optimal when managed under the traditional approaches. A new approach, which recognizes these phenomena and allows for them, is needed so we may better manage our factories.

The Production Dice Game was developed by Dr. Eliyahu M. Goldratt, author of The Goal[1].

The Production Dice game has been developed in order to illustrate the effects of Dependent Events and Statistical Fluctuations on a manufacturing operation and to understand ways to deal with them.

The game is played by creating a simple manufacturing operation. The material processed by this plant can be represented by any readily available product in the factory. It is best to use products produced in your own plant as this will help relate the lessons of the game to your environment. The only requirement for the material you choose to use is that it be something that can be set on a table and people can move it easily. You will need several hundred pieces of this material to play the game. A team of 6 to 8 players is set up to represent 6 to 8 sequential operations required to process the material (see Figure). If there are more than 8 players, it is better to arrange them as several independent product lines of 5-8 people each. More complicated production flows can be represented, but the basic effects of Dependent Events and Statistical Fluctuations are very well illustrated by this simple linear production line making just one product.

Figure 1

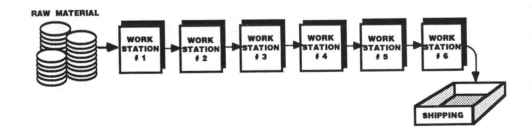

Each player represents a work station. He processes the material by moving them from his left to his right. The next player/work station (the player to his right) can then process these pieces and move them to his right. When the pieces have been processed by the last player on the right they are ready to be shipped.

The Dependent Events in this game are obvious: pieces cannot move on to work station 2 without first passing through work station 1 and so on.

Ordinary dice are used to create the effect of fluctuations. Each player/work station is given a die. The roll of the die is used to represent the actual productive capability of each work station on a given day. A low role of the die (such as 1) represents a day plagued with breakdowns, absenteeism, accidents and similar problems. A high role of the die (such as 6) represents a good day with few problems and a high output potential for that work station. The random and unpredictable nature of the problems we encounter in our plants is represented by the random nature of the outcome of a roll of the die. However, over a number of rolls the average outcome should be 3.5 (Since each number between 1 and 6 is equally probable). Thus the average production capability of each work station is 3.5 units per day.

Figure 2

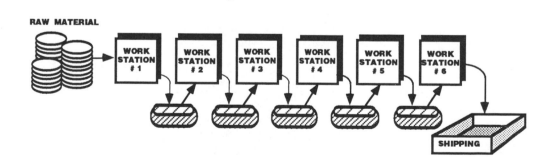

Playing The Game   One toss of the die constitutes one day's production at the work station. After the toss the player/work station moves forward (processes - see Figure 2) the number of pieces indicated by the die.

If the die toss exceeds the number of pieces available in work-in-process at the beginning of the day, then only move forward the pieces that are available. Do not use the pieces processed at the preceding work station the same day; this is tomorrow's work queue. It is therefore possible that a work station cannot produce to its capacity due to the lack of material, a situation that is a common occurrence in a real manufacturing plant, as lost production time.

Set up the game with an initial work-in-process queue of four pieces at each work station (Since this represents more than an average day's production). The first operation is the only exception. There is an adequate supply of material to cover the full month's work. See Figure 3 for a pictorial representation.

Figure 3

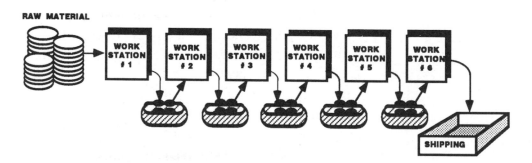

With this setup it appears that the plant(or production line) should have no difficulty meeting a market demand of 70 units per month.

AVERAGE PRODUCTION CAPACITY = 3.5 UNITS PER DAY
NUMBER OF WORKING DAYS IN AN AVERAGE MONTH = 20 DAYS
EXPECTED PRODUCTION CAPACITY = 20 X 3.5 = 70 UNITS.

Of course, the production will not be 3.5 units every single day. There will be good days when it will be more than 3.5 units and there will be bad days when it will be less than 3.5 units. But over the course of the 20 days /20 tosses of the die, the plant expects to produce 70 units.

Also, since the average capacity of each work station is the same (3.5 units/da) and since this matches exactly what we need (market demand = 70 units in 20 days) we seem to have a simple job of managing this plant !!

A single product manufactured in a few operations, where the capacity of each work station is exactly equal to the demand of the market, represents an apparently easily managed manufacturing model.

The only problem appears to be the random production of each work station. While this may cause some temporary problems, we expect these to average out.

Or Will They ?

*Measuring
Performance*

The performance of the plant / team and that of each operation are recorded in the forms provided. The actual roll is the number on the die for that day, representing daily production. The pieces processed is the number of pieces actually moved to the next work station. This number cannot exceed the actual roll of the die. The efficiency of the work station is the ratio of pieces processed to the actual roll. The work-in-process is the queue inventory in front of the work station /player at the end of each day after the player has completed moving his material and has received material from the previous work station. This should give us the information necessary to identify which operation is responsible for unsatisfactory performance. A sample form has been filled out as an example (see Figure 4).

When you look at the results, you will find that the performance of this simple one-product production line to be well below expectations.

- Total shipments for the month are significantly lower than the 70 units expected.
- The inventory at the end of the 20 days is significantly higher than the starting inventory.

The inescapable phenomena of Dependent Events and Statistical Fluctuations have combined to cause this poor performance. At the beginning it looked like a simple plant. At the end it resembles a real-life plant, with randomly distributed piles of inventory and with difficulty in making shipments. If this is the degree to which these two phenomena impact such a simple environment, you can imagine what they can do to more complex real-life environments.

Dice Game Score Sheet

Operational Performance - For Work Station # 4

Roll No. = Day	Actual Roll	Pieces Processed	Efficiency %	WIP	Overtime Rolls
1 2 3 4 5	5 3 3 5 3	4 3 2 1 3	80 100 67 20 100	4 2 1 4 3	
Week 1 Averages	3.8	2.6	68	3	
6 7 8 9 10	1 6 1 4 4	1 4 1 4 4	100 67 100 100 100	4 4 6 7 4	
Week 2 Averages	3.2	2.8	88	7	

Week	Expected Shipments (cumulative)	Actual Shipments	Past Due Shipments	Inventory	Overtime
1	17.5	14	3.5	18	
2	35	27	8	23	

Dice Game Score Sheet

Operational Performance - For Work Station _____

Roll No. = Day	Actual Roll	Pieces Processed	Efficiency %	WIP	Overtime Rolls
1 2 3 4 5					
Week 1 Averages					
6 7 8 9 10					
Week 2 Averages					

Week	Expected Shipments (cumulative)	Actual Shipments	Past Due Shipments	Inventory	Overtime
1					
2					

Dice Game Score Sheet

Operational Performance - For Work Station _____

Roll No. = Day	Actual Roll	Pieces Processed	Efficiency %	WIP	Overtime Rolls
10 12 13 14 15					
Week 1 Averages					
16 17 18 19 20					
Week 2 Averages					

Plant/Team Performance

Week	Expected Shipments (cumulative)	Actual Shipments	Past Due Shipments	Inventory	Overtime
1					
2					
Monthly Totals					

VARIATIONS OF THE BASIC DICE GAME

1. USE OF OVERTIME :

Whenever the production output is less than the expected or required amount, we resort to the use of overtime. However, this is done in a reactionary fashion and does not improve the shipments to the degree expected. The concept of overtime can be incorporated into the game, by allowing any one player/work station an additional role of the die after everyone has completed production for a given day.

To play this variation appoint one person as the plant manager. He is responsible for deciding who uses the available overtime. Set a limit of five to ten overtime rolls for the plant as a whole during the 20 days. Overtime rolls are recorded in the column provided on the score sheet. Note that the work in process of the next work station (the one following the operator with overtime) will have to be updated. For each additional role of overtime, deduct the revenue equivalent of one piece from the shipments. The plant manager is responsible for the total shipments, the total inventory and the overtime used. See how well the plant now performs !!

2. THE UNBALANCED PLANT :

A manufacturing operation in which the available capacity at different resources is not exactly matched with the market demand and in which the available capacity at different resources (as a function of the market demand) is different, is an unbalanced plant. All real-life manufacturing operations are unbalanced. What is the effect of Statistical Fluctuations and Dependent Events in an unbalanced plant?

To see the effects of Statistical Fluctuations and Dependent Events in an unbalanced plant, you can modify the dice game set up to represent an unbalanced plant. The simplest and easiest way to change the capacity balance that exists in the game setup is to provide some of the resources with more than one die. Any resource that has two available dice, for example, has the capacity to produce seven units per day. Set up the Production Dice Game so that one player (resource) has one die and all other players have two dice. Start with the one die at the end of the production process (the last player).

Play the game as before and see what happens to the T, I and OE of this plant.

Change the location of the single die in the production process. Play a number of different variations in which the player with the single die is in the middle of the process and at the end.

Document the results for all of the different variations you play on the form provided for future reference.

<u>The Production Dice Game</u>   Variation # _____

Title ————————————————   Date   ————————————

Description: _____

_____

_____

_____

Setup:

RAW MATERIAL

WORK STATION #1   WORK STATION #2   WORK STATION #3   WORK STATION #4   WORK STATION #5   WORK STATION #6

SHIPPING

_____

_____

_____

Playing Rules: _____

_____

_____

Conclusions: _____

_____

_____

Appendix C
Setting The Production Batch Size

In this book it has been the thesis that traditional approaches to decision-making in manufacturing organizations must be replaced. This is because they are totally focussed on cost and efficiency and not on the other competitive elements such as production lead times, reliable deliveries, new products, quality and so on. The approach used by most manufacturing companies to determine the *batch sizes* for production in their facilities is no different. Batch sizing serves as an excellent example for the above thesis. We will also see in this appendix how the concepts of Synchronous Manufacturing can be used to approach this issue of selecting production batch sizes.

The traditional approach to setting the proper batch size consists of trying to minimize the production cost of the batch. Too large a batch will increase the carrying cost by increasing the inventory level and too small a batch will increase the cost of setups. The proper batch size is one that will provide a compromise between these two extremes. A wide assortment of techniques is available to refine the ability to determine the best batch size for any given situation. However, the problem manufacturing companies face in using this approach to setting batch (or lot) sizes is not that they do not use the best technique for their specific case. Rather, the problem they face is that the objective of the approach is misplaced. The size of the batch influences more than the inventories and setups. Yet, the traditional approach ignores these other non-cost elements and focusses entirely on minimizing the production cost.

To understand how to determine the proper batch size, we must understand the full impact of batch sizes. When batch sizes are reduced, the inventory in the system goes down. In fact, the inventory in the system is directly proportional to the size of the batch. Also, as the batch size is reduced and the inventory decreases, the production lead time decreases proportionately. To see this relationship between production batches and lead times, consider the three-step process depicted in Figure C 1.

FIGURE C 1

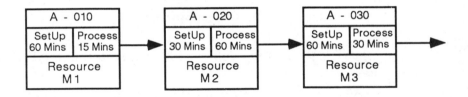

Figure C 2 shows the movement of a production batch of 40 units. The lead time as can be seen in the figure is 72.5 hours. In Figure C 3, we see the movement of a batch of half the size, and the lead time is 37.5 hours. The same argument holds true in more complex production flows. In more complex cases, as Jonah points out, the total lead time for a batch consists of four elements:

1. Production time
2. Setup time
3. Queue time
4. Wait time

When the batch size is reduced by half, the production time is clearly reduced by half. The setup is unaffected. However, both the queue and wait times are reduced by half. The queue time is reduced by half because the production time on the batches ahead of the particular batch is now half as long.

FIGURE C 2

Process Batch = 40 Pieces

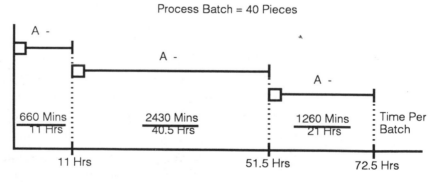

Manufacturing Cycle Time MCT

The setup time which is unaffected is usually a small percentage of the production time. Thus the overall reduction in queue time is almost one half. The same argument will show that the wait time is also reduced by half when the production batch is reduced by half. Thus, when the production is reduced by half, the overall production lead time is reduced by half.

FIGURE C 3

Process Batch = 20 Pieces

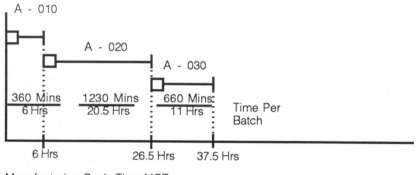

Manufacturing Cycle Time MCT

As we saw in Chapter Nine the benefits from a reduced production lead time are very significant.[7] (pp. 36-66) In fact, most competitive elements are favorably influenced by a reduction in production lead time. The saving in carrying cost realized from the reduced inventory may, in many cases, be the least significant benefit. Yet, this is the only tangible benefit recognized by the traditional approach. From a purely competitive standpoint, the smaller the production batch size, the better.

The approach used in Synchronous Manufacturing is in strong contrast to the traditional approach, where we start with the basic assumption that the larger the production batch size, the better (since setup costs can be amortized over more units). In trying to minimize the calculated production costs we end up with the largest batch size with which we can manage to survive. While setup costs are low, there is a long list of hidden costs (lack of flexibility to demand changes, difficulty of identifying quality problems, larger facilities and equipment to handle the chaos, etc.) that in the end make the production facility non-competitive. The traditional approach will lead to a low unit cost mode of production that is, as a result, non-competitive.

Synchronous Manufacturing, in contrast to the cost view, is focussed on the competitive elements of the operation. In this approach, we start with the extremely small batch sizes and work our way grudgingly, to the smallest batch with which we can operate. There is only one drawback to working with small batches. Smaller batches may require more setups at key resources and this may result in lost production time. Traditional approaches have assumed that this is always the case. They have, therefore, assumed that every setup will add to the cost of production. However, this assumption is not always true. Smaller production batches will not always result in lost production time due to two important factors:

1. Most resources in most manufacturing operations are in the Non-Bottleneck category. They have excess capacity available. Increasing the number of setups will result in a real loss of production only after the excess capacity has been depleted. As long as excess capacity exists, the opportunity for reducing the size of the production batch exists. The only resource where an increase in setups will cause a loss of Throughput is the Bottleneck resource. A Bottleneck resource has no excess capacity available and any increase in setup will result in lost Throughput. Conversely, any decrease in setup (either by reducing the setup times or increasing the batch sizes) will create an opportunity for increasing the Throughput of the entire system. In determining the batch size the nature of the resource, whether it is a Bottleneck or not, should be considered.

2. Smaller production batches do not necessarily mean an increase in the number of setups. This counter-intuitive result is due to the fact that when we operate with large batches, the material moves through the system in waves with large and unpredictable lead times. When the lead times are large, demand fluctuations are more likely. Both the wave-like production and the changing demand increase the need to expedite material. This expediting inevitably results in unplanned setups. Thus, with large batch sizes there is a considerable number of unplanned setups caused by the very nature of working with large batches. Smaller batches result in smoother flow of material and the production lead times are shorter. The need to expedite is greatly reduced and so are the number of unplanned setups. When we take into account the unplanned setups, the number of actual setups done on the factory floor, with large and with small batches, may end up being the same.

Given the overwhelming advantages of smaller batches, we should always work with the smallest possible batch (not the largest possible batch). The only area where we should even consider increasing batch sizes is at the Bottleneck resources. In fact, the logical conclusion of this discussion is that:[8]

The Production Batch should not be the same at all operations, even for a given product.

We can further impact the production lead time by borrowing some practices from the assembly line. In most manufacturing operations, where the different processes are not physically connected to one another (with pipes, conveyors etc.) the usual practice is to move material from one resource to the next in quantities equal to the production batch size. We wait for the first work center to complete processing the entire batch before it is moved to the second resource. This, of course, reduces the material handling costs. However, if we analyze any of the process or flow type operations we find that their practices are entirely different. Consider, for example, the assembly line. Since assembly lines are dedicated to the production of a single type of product and changeovers are not frequent, it is safe to assert that the production batch is extremely large. The material is not allowed to accumulate between two stages of the assembly line. Each piece is moved from one stage to the next. In fact, the ability to do this is the raison d'ietre of the assembly line. In the case of the assembly line, overall production lead times are short, in spite of the large production batches, because the material moves from station to station in very small quantities.

We should recognize that there are two distinct batch sizes under discussion here:[8]

1. The Production Batch or Process Batch: This is the usual concept of lot size and refers to the number of units produced at a resource between two setups of that resource.

2. The Transfer Batch or Move Quantity: This is the number of units that will be moved from resource to resource.

In the case of the assembly line, for example, the Process Batch is very large while the Transfer Batch is very small (one).

For a given choice of the Process Batch, we can reduce the production lead time by reducing the size of the Transfer Batch. To see this, consider the simple production process shown in Figure C1. If the Process Batch of 40 is processed as a single Transfer Batch, the material moves through the system as shown in Figure C 2. If the Process Batch of 40 is moved from operation to operation in quantities of 10, i.e. if the Transfer Batch is set to 10, then the movement of material through the system is shown in Figure C 4.

FIGURE C 4

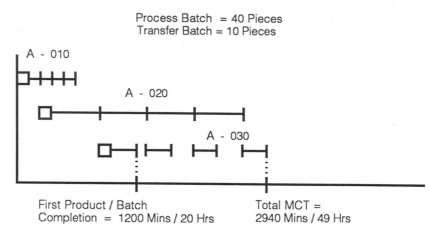

Process Batch = 40 Pieces
Transfer Batch = 10 Pieces

A - 010

A - 020

A - 030

First Product / Batch
Completion = 1200 Mins / 20 Hrs

Total MCT =
2940 Mins / 49 Hrs

Clearly, the use of the Transfer Batch results in much shorter lead times. What is particularly noteworthy about this reduced lead time is that the number of setups is exactly the same in both cases, Figure C 2 and Figure C 4. This is summarized by the following principle of Synchronous Manufacturing:[8]

The Transfer Batch and The Process Batch need not, and most often should not, be the same.

Appendix D
References

1. Eliyahu M. Goldratt and Jeff Cox
    The Goal
    North River Press, Inc., 1984.

2. Robert H. Hayes and Steven C. Wheelwright
    Restoring Our Competitive Edge
    John Wiley & Sons, Inc., 1984.

3. Wickham Skinner
    Manufacturing: The Formidable Competitive Weapon
    John Wiley & Sons, Inc., 1985.

4. Robert S. Kaplan
    "Yesterday's Production Undermines Production"
    The Harvard Business Review, Vol. 62
    (July - August 1984, pp. 95).

5. Robert S. Kaplan
    "Measuring Manufacturing Performance"
    The Accounting Review, Vol. LVIII
    No.4 (October 1983).

6. Roger Schmenner
    "Every Factory Has A Life Cycle"
    The Harvard Business Review
    (March - April 1983).

7. Eliyahu M. Goldratt and Robert Fox
    The Race
    North River Press, Inc., 1986.

8. Robert Fox
    "MRP, Kanban or OPT: What's Best?"
    Inventories and Production Magazine
    (July - August 1982).

9. Mokshagundam L. Srikanth and Michael Umble
    Synchronous Manufacturing: Principles for World-Class Excellence
    Southwestern Publishing Co. and
    The Spectrum Publishing Co., Inc. 1989.

10. Woody Woodson
    "Perspectives - Back To The Future"
    Management Accounting, Vol. LXVIII
    (11 May 1987).

About The Authors

Mokshagundam L. Srikanth, PhD, and Harold E. Cavallaro, Jr. have been intimately involved with the development and implementation of Synchronous Manufacturing since these concepts were introduced to the United States in 1979.

Prior to founding The Spectrum Management Group, Inc., both worked closely with the author of *The Goal,* Dr. Eliyahu Goldratt. Dr. Srikanth was Senior Research Fellow and Director of Operations and Mr. Cavallaro was Director of Education at Creative Output, Inc., the organization founded by Dr. Goldratt.

Authors Srikanth and Cavallaro have played a major role in the development and refinement of the concepts and techniques of Synchronous Manufacturing. They have implemented these tecniques in over thirty companies and have organized and delivered the education, training and consulting services to support these projects.

Their experience covers a broad cross-section of industries including; Automotive, Agricultural, Aerospace & Defense, Electronics, Industrial and Consumer Tools & Equipment and Textile Industries.

Both authors have spoken widely on Synchronous Manufacturing and issues arising from its application within the academic, societal and business community.

Other Publications
on the subject of
Synchronous Manufacturing...

The following pages contain information on related texts published by The Spectrum Publishing Company, Inc.

The Synchronous Manufacturing Bookshop, A Division of The Spectrum Publishing Company, Inc., currently carries a comprehensive selection of texts relative to this dynamic management technology.

Action Item!

For our latest brochure, and ordering information, contact:
- The Spectrum Publishing Company, Inc.
  300 Landmark Center, 1062 Barnes Road
  Wallingford, CT 06492
  (203) 284-1944

Synchronous Manufacturing:
Principles for World-Class Excellence

* By Umble & Srikanth
* 270 Pages.
* Softcover.

Business and academic professionals alike have endorsed this work as the most comprehensive text available on the subject of Synchronous Manufacturing.

Why does the standard cost system fail?...and what new strategies and principles need to be applied in managing manufactuing operations? *Synchronous Manufacturing: Principles for World-Class Excellence* offers eye-opening insight, providing the student and the practitioner with an understanding of fundamental issues in manufacturing management and the ability to analyze and improve manufacturing operations.

A stellar example of practical application experience and scholarly thesis, this text combines case studies, application aids and vital information heretofore unavailable in printed form.

Action Item!

> "...this is the first book that can really do the job of informing production and operations managers of the know-how of Synchronous Manufacturing."
> * Eliyahu Goldratt
>   Author, *The Goal*

The WORKBOOK
Synchronous Manufacturing:
Principles for World-Class Excellence

- By Srikanth & Podzunas
- 64 Pages.
- Softcover.

The answers to the end-of-chapter questions and more! Contributing to this helpful companion to the outstanding textbook *Synchronous Manufacturing: Principles for World Class Excellence,* Albert E. Podzunas gets you thinking with the sections entitled "From Principle to Practice". Mr. Podzunas is one of the leading implementers of the process of Synchronous Manufacturing, and a partner in The Spectrum Management Group, Inc.

Also included is a brief summary of each chapter of the text, highlighting important points for discussion.

Action Item!

> Far more than your average workbook; this text could have been called a "Guidebook."
> - Order today !

Regaining Control:
Get Me To The Shipping Dock on Time!

- By Burgess & Srikanth
- Two Volumes
- 269 Pages.
- Softcover.
- Includes MS-DOS compatible software.

The transformation of traditional managerial thinking to the concepts of Synchronous Manufacturing is vital if improvements are to be sustained. *Regaining Control,* written in novel form, illustrates the concepts of Synchronous Manufacturing and their interactions as they are applied at "Tyger Auto Company, Inc."

This instructional case study comes complete with software which transforms the reader to "Operations Manager" in order to test the effectiveness of the strategic decisions he or she would make. Serious students and practitioners of Synchronous Manufacturing will find this package to be a significant aid in the conversion of concept to reality.

Action Item!

> "...presents the concepts of Synchronous Manufacturing in such a manner as to make them universally applicable..."
> - Dave Wilke
>   Divisional Synchronous Coordinator
>   General Motors Corporation,
>   Saginaw Division

For More Information

The Spectrum Management Group, Inc., can provide the expertise to take you beyond *The Goal* and *Regaining Competitiveness,* toward implementation of Synchronous Manufacturing management techniques throughout your manufacturing operations.

Through analysis, in close cooperation with your staff, we can assist you in the identification of the specific application of these techniques within your operations. Once the application has been identified we can help your management team translate the analysis into a detailed implementation program and show you how to apply these techniques.

Working closely with you during the implementation through consulting support, management education and training programs, we can help you move rapidly toward a successful and long term implementation of Synchronous Manufacturing management techniques at all levels of your organization.

Action Item!

> For more information on the concepts and implementation of the principles presented in this publication contact:
> * Mr. Graham Side
>   The Spectrum Management Group, Inc.
>   300 Landmark Center • 1062 Barnes Road
>   Wallingford, CT 06492
>   (203) 284- 8998

The Response ...

- "This book is mandatory reading for all manufacturing people."

> William R. Harris
> Senior Vice President & CMO
> Convergent Technologies

- "*Regaining Competitiveness* is an excellent extension of *The Goal*. We plan to use *Regaining Competitiveness* to educate our people at all levels to understand the concepts and have a working knowledge of the methodologies that made *The Goal* such an important text."

> Charles W. Denny
> Vice President Electrical Group
> Square D Company

- "Conceptual transfer at its best. Fully implemented, this catalytic book blasts you into the future as a formidable competitor. A must read."

> Robert G. Widham
> Group Vice President
> The Stanley Works

- " I believe the authors have performed a distinct service in publishing *Regaining Competitiveness* since it descibes in very specific terms how to put the principles outlined in *The Goal* to work."

  M. William Grant
  Vice President - Technology
  Ingersoll-Rand Company

- " *Regaining Competitiveness* presents and reinforces a valuable message for anyone responsible for improving manufacturing productivity ...must reading."

  James I Morgan, CAE
  President
  National Fluid Power Association

- " The format of the book is excellent. *Regaining Competitiveness* takes the basic material from *The Goal* and translates it for manufacturing managers, and of course controllers, into directly workable concepts."

  Alfred M. King
  Managing Director Professional Services
  National Association of Accountants

- "If American industry is going to recover and respond to international competition the principles and lessons taught here must be learned and applied posthaste."

  Gene Myers
  President
  Megadiamond, Smith Industries, Inc.

- *"Regaining Competitiveness* is an excellent, hands-on tool for implementing the advanced manufacturing concepts in *The Goal* within your own organization. Practical. Implementable."

  Robert Vanoureck
  Group Vice President
  Mailing Systems
  Pitney Bowes

- "I commend the authors for their ability to cut through the perceived problems and address the real issues. It is what many of us with years of experience in manufacturing have been looking for."

  Joseph P Handerhan
  Manager Manufacturing Operations
  Ingersol - Rand Company, Rock Drill Division
  Winners of The 1986 U.S. Senate Productivity Award

- "An excellent overall analysis of the principles introduced by *The Goal.* Good easy reading that brings the principles directly into your own business."

  Duncan D. Sutphen
  Vice President Operations
  Dresser Pump Division, Dresser Industries, Inc.